Managing Performance for Results

A Four-Phase Approach

Peter C. Joseph

Printed in the United States of America

First Printing, August 2016

Peake Human Capital Consulting

www.PeakeHumanCapital.com

ISBN: 1523479493
ISBN 13: 9781523479498

Contents

Introduction

In mid-2006, I was hired by a major media company to design and implement a process for documenting the company's most important business objectives, communicating them at all levels and across all departments, and creating and tracking departmental and individual goals aligned with company objectives. In addition, the process had to provide a fair and objective annual appraisal for each team member and a means for developing the skills team members needed to achieve current and future objectives.

This was no small feat. The company's performance management landscape was like the wild wild west. There was no real company strategy, and what there was of it was not communicated beyond the senior management level. The vast majority of team members had no idea what the company needed to accomplish during the upcoming year or how their individual work or the work of their departments contributed to it. Team members did not have clear, documented performance expectations. Performance appraisals were inconsistent. In one department, they were based almost entirely on feedback from peers. In another, they were written in glowing prose that, in most cases, overemphasized team members' accomplishments while ignoring areas in which they underperformed. In general, performance appraisals were completed in whatever way managers chose, varying from simple checklists to sticky notes reading "Good job this year—I'm giving you a five-percent raise." More than fifty appraisal templates were being used, resulting in an inconsistent process that team members perceived as unfair and—in many cases—demoralizing. Worse yet, there was no way to look at actual performance across the company to determine how we were performing as a whole and how we needed to adjust performance to achieve objectives.

This was a real problem. Like most media companies at the time, we were not performing well financially and faced the very real possibility of significantly shrinking or going out of business altogether. We needed a way to quickly get clear about our most critical business objectives and to get all of our people—from the C suite to the mailroom—to align their everyday work with these objectives.

As I embarked on researching, designing, and implementing this performance management process, it became clear that the few managers in our ranks who consistently set clear expectations, provided regular feedback on performance toward those expectations, wrote fair appraisals based on performance, and provided opportunities for professional development and growth had better-than-average departmental performance and considerably higher team-member engagement. My mission was to expand these effective practices throughout the company.

Nearly a decade later, the performance management process has become an integral part of how the company does business. Senior executives and managers have expressed that it gives them an effective way to communicate expectations and track individual and departmental performance toward them. Team members have expressed that it provides clarity on performance expectations and removes much of the subjectivity from the appraisal process while giving them a voice in it.

Most importantly, virtually every team member is now clear on the company's most critical business objectives and on what they need to do to contribute to achieving them.

My mission now is to help as many managers as possible—beyond my organization—achieve the results they desire through effectively managing performance. The knowledge and tools needed are on the pages that follow.

Peter Joseph
Peake Human Capital Consulting, LLC

How to Use This Toolkit

This toolkit is designed to be practical. It contains the minimal amounts of theory and explanation you will need to understand the important concepts but is focused largely on providing the step-by-step guidance and accompanying tools you need to effectively manage performance within you organization right now.

I recommend two approaches for using this toolkit most effectively. The first is to read each section and use the accompanying tools to implement each phase of the process as you go. The second—and more highly recommended—approach is to read the entire toolkit, reflect on it for a week or so, discuss it with your manager, and then implement the process using the accompanying tools.

The toolkit is divided into four main sections, each focusing on a specific phase of the performance management process. Each section contains a brief overview of the phase, expected outcomes after you implement the phase, and step-by-step guidance on how to implement the phase—including all of the basic tools needed.

This toolkit is meant to provide a basic, effective performance management platform. I strongly recommend that as you use it, you consider your company's culture and politics and that you make adjustments as needed. It's like following a recipe in a cookbook. As long as you follow the basic recipe, you can make a few minor changes to the ingredients to create a dish that most effectively suits your needs.

Why Bother with Performance Management?

"Why bother with performance management?" I get that question all the time—well, not so much in those words, but through the resistance that many managers, even the most well-meaning, often show during the process.

"I don't have time…No one else is doing it…I've gotten along OK so far without it…I'll get to it when I can…" I hear that over and over from managers, especially during the first year or two of a performance management process implementation. As the process matures and managers execute it (some of them kicking and screaming), the majority of them build the good performance management habits that eventually get them the results they want to achieve in less time and with fewer headaches along the way. Because of this, many of the managers who were most resistant to the process in the beginning are now its biggest promoters.

Truth be told, performance management is conceptually simple, but simple does not always mean easy. Think of working out at the gym to get in shape. Is it simple? Yes. But is it easy? For most of us, the answer is, not always. Working out at the gym, however, consists of a series of simple behaviors done to the best of our ability on a regular basis over time. The same is true for managing performance. Follow this approach while working out at the gym and you will develop a strong, fit, healthier, and more attractive body. Follow it while managing performance and you will develop a strong, fit, more competent, and more productive team and organization.

The Business Case for Performance Management

Research shows that organizations that implement and execute effective performance management processes outperform their peers. When designed and managed well, a performance management process enables an organization to

- document and communicate the most important company business objectives;
- communicate company business objectives to all team members;
- create, document, and communicate departmental and individual objectives that support company business objectives;
- focus all team members on doing work that will advance company business objectives;
- track individual, departmental, and company performance toward objectives; and
- determine where performance is excelling or underperforming and make adjustments as needed.

In addition, team members who know their companies' most important business objectives and who have clear expectations about what they need to do to support those objectives are more engaged, more satisfied with their jobs, and, as a as a whole, provide more discretionary effort to their work than other team members.

The Cost of Poor Performance Management

Conversely, organizations that do a poor job of managing performance—not setting clear expectations, giving performance feedback too infrequently, not appraising based on performance toward documented goals, and not providing team members with growth and development opportunities—risk creating work environments rife with inefficiencies, unfocused efforts, disengaged team members, and higher turnover, which result in a decidedly negative impact on bottom-line results.

How Do I Make This Work If I'm Not the Boss?

"I'm still waiting for my boss to give me goals. I can't manage my own performance." I still hear that from a handful of team members every year. It's a cop out. Yes, you *can* manage your own performance—at least to an extent—and it's in your best interest to do so if your boss doesn't take the lead.

If you are waiting for your boss to set and track your performance goals, ask yourself these questions: "Do I want to risk getting a performance appraisal that doesn't reflect my achievements? Do I want my appraisal to be subjective and based on what is in the boss's recent memory? Do I want my appraisal to be an unpleasant surprise?" Your answer to these questions, of course, is no. You are likely, however, to face these situations at appraisal time if you don't take the lead and prompt your boss to manage your performance.

There are many reasons why bosses don't take the time to manage performance: their teams are large; they are swamped and don't seem to have the time; they just don't think performance management is necessary. These, too, are cop outs. Again, it's like going to the gym to get in shape. To make it work and get results, you've got to schedule the time and take the necessary actions to build the habits that get results. It may feel time consuming and labor intensive at first, but once the habits are established and it becomes part of the fabric of everyday life, the process is much easier and much less time consuming.

If your boss doesn't set clear expectations for you at the beginning of your performance year, use the expectation setting section of this book (see page 1) to think through and create your own. Then contact your boss and request a meeting, phone call, or—as a last resort—e-mail exchange to review, revise, and approve your goals and competencies. Request regular meetings—at least monthly, but preferably weekly or every other week—to review progress toward your performance expectations, receive feedback, and get the coaching you need to get back on track if you have veered off course. You will perform better throughout the year and will be in a much better position to receive a fair, objective appraisal based on your actual performance toward established expectations.

The Software Myth

"Don't I need software to run a performance management process?" This question comes up frequently, too. While software is definitely a useful tool, especially for managing performance across a large organization and running analytics, don't let the lack of it stop you. Executing sound, effective performance management practices is the most important thing. Doing that with an Excel spreadsheet or Access database will produce better results than not doing it at all. A solid performance management process is far more important than fancy performance management software.

In recent years, I have seen more than one company buy expensive performance management software without first designing a solid performance management process. Every one of these companies is still struggling to make their performance management processes work. They assumed that the software alone, once introduced to managers and team members, would suffice as a performance management process and get results. That's like buying a high-tech race car and assuming managers will drive it effectively once you put them behind the wheel. The most important thing is to make sure managers know how to drive and to guide them through that process. Once they know how to drive, you can put them behind the wheel of a Chevrolet or a Lamborghini, and they will know what to do.

There are many companies providing performance management software today. There are options for companies of any size as well as options for any budget. If you are interested in purchasing software, it is imperative that you design your performance management process first (the tools provided in this book will help). After designing your process, determine the functionality the software must have to support it. Finally, choose software that meets these needs. Make sure the software supports your process, not the other way around.

On a final note, the purpose of performance management software is to document organizational, departmental, and individual goals in one place; track performance toward those goals; and provide organization-wide data on performance toward goals. For that reason, performance management software should, ideally, be implemented across an entire organization.

The Four Critical Phases of Performance Management

Whether you are using elaborate software, an Excel spreadsheet, or pen and paper, your performance management process must have four critical phases to be effective. These phases are

1. set expectations,

2. review progress,

3. appraise performance, and

4. plan your development.

Phase One: Set Expectations

Expectations consist of objectives and competencies (the knowledge, skills, and behaviors necessary to effectively achieve objectives). In this phase, managers set overall goals for their departments (these also become the manager's goals). Then, managers collaborate with their team members to set their individual goals and competencies. All goals should support—directly or indirectly—departmental and company goals.

Phase Two: Review Progress

During this ongoing phase, managers and their team members track progress toward individual goals and record performance notes to use on the performance appraisal later in the year. If desired, managers also complete quarterly or midyear appraisals of their team members. Performance expectations set earlier in the year are revised as needed to reflect current business needs.

Phase Three: Appraise Performance

Managers complete annual performance appraisals for each of their team members. Ideally, team members should have the option of completing self-appraisals to give them a voice in the process and to promote a sense of involvement and fairness. Appraisals include ratings and comments on goals and competencies established during the year. Performance notes collected during the year are used to justify ratings given.

Phase Four: Plan Your Development

Team members and their managers create optional development plans geared toward enhancing competencies—the knowledge, skills, and abilities needed for successful achievement of business goals or for career growth.

These four phases work together in a cyclical, ongoing process that ensures clarity of expectations, focus on what is most important, accurate feedback, course correction when needed, and development of skills needed for ongoing success. Skipping any of the phases is like removing one of the four tires from a car. Don't do it. You won't like the result.

Phase One: Set Expectations

Desired Outcomes

- Four to eight clear, written departmental or team goals representing at least 90 percent of what the department or team is responsible for accomplishing

- Four to eight clear, written individual goals for each team member, representing at least 90 percent of his or her job

- Clear, written competencies (knowledge, skills, and behaviors required for success) for each team member

- Goals and competencies accessible to team members throughout the performance year

"Why go to the trouble of formally setting expectations? We're all busy, and it's so time consuming. My people know what to do, and they are already performing well. If they mess up, I'll let them know." I hear this more times than I can count from managers at all levels. My response to them has always been *"Pay now or pay later."*

Not setting, documenting, and communicating clear expectations is like setting off on a road trip without a clear plan. If you want your team to drive from the east coast to the west coast of a large country, you have two options: throw them all into a van and say, "Drive west—follow the sunset," or set some clear expectations that get everyone pulling together toward that common goal. In this option you would do things like

- determine which specific west coast city will be your destination;

- determine how long it will take you to reach that city; and

- determine who will plan the route, who will drive, who will navigate, who will be responsible for meals, who will book hotel accommodations, and so forth. For each of these responsibilities, you would be clear about what successful performance would look like (plan and follow the shortest route to the destination city, drive three hundred miles per day, ensure that each team member has three nutritious meals per day, etc.).

Could you get to the west coast by throwing your team into a van and telling them to follow the sunset? Yes, you could, but the journey would likely be longer, more difficult, more expensive, and less pleasant.

A few years ago, I had a conversation with a manager about setting expectations for her team members. During the conversation, she made it clear that she thought this was an unnecessary waste of time. The conversation went something like this:

Manager: Why should I set and track expectations for my team members? They don't need goals. Their goal is to do their job.

Me: How do you know that your idea of "doing their job" and their idea of "doing their job" are the same idea?

Manager: It's obvious. They do their jobs every day. They know what they are supposed to do.

Me:	But how do you know how well they are really performing throughout the entire year? How do you make sure they are staying on track? How do you write performance appraisals that accurately reflect the work they did throughout the entire year?
Manager:	I hold information about their performance in my head. When they're not performing well, I tell them.

Later that year, the company's legal department contacted me. The manager's team had become dysfunctional. Team members were feuding with one another. Work was slowing down. Targets were being missed. Deliverables were often late. One of the team members filed a grievance and, as part of the settlement, I was asked to intervene to help the manager create a more cohesive, functional team.

After a lengthy meeting with the manager and the team to identify the issues and their root causes, I had a debriefing conversation with her. It went something like this:

Me:	So what are your thoughts after meeting with the team?
Manager:	(Sigh) Wow. That was really sobering. It's clear now that most of the issues my team brought up have to do with how I have been managing them. I need to change my approach
Me:	In what ways?
Manager:	Well, first of all, I'm not communicating with them clearly and frequently enough. I thought they knew what I expected of them, but it's clear they don't. I need to be clearer and more specific about their performance expectations, and I need to make sure they are written down somewhere where we can refer to them throughout the year. We need to be able to make revisions, too, when we need them.
Me:	Good. What other ideas do you have?
Manager:	I also need to give them feedback more often. They told me that I only give them feedback when they mess up, so I need to let them know when they do a good job, too.
Me:	That's another good idea.
Manager:	They also told me that I left some of their accomplishments off their appraisals and that I added goals to their appraisals while I was writing them. They were upset that I had not told them about these goals until appraisal time and that I gave them low marks for not accomplishing them the way I wanted. I need to set expectations early in the year, give balanced feedback throughout the year, and write their appraisals based on that. They also said they feel like they are in a rut and want the chance to learn new skills…
Me:	(Silently, to myself) She just decided to use the process she has been resisting for so long…and that's *great*!

Again, the moral of the story is, pay now or pay later. A little time and planning up front leads to a smoother journey and, in almost every case, far better results.

Setting Clear Expectations: Some Additional Wisdom

"Will you please tell me which way I ought to go from here?"

"That depends a good deal on where you want to get to," said the Cat.

"I don't much care where…" said Alice.

"Then it doesn't matter which way you go," said the Cat.

—*Alice in Wonderland*, Lewis Carroll

The way to achieve success is first, have a definite, clear practical ideal; a goal, an objective. Second, have the necessary means to achieve your ends; wisdom, money, materials, and methods. Third, adjust all your means to that end.

—Aristotle

The bottom line for us as leaders is that we get results.

To succeed in a rapidly changing world, we need to be crystal clear about what those results are.

Begin with the end in mind.

—Stephen Covey

The Most Effective Goals Align with Company Strategy

Alignment is one of the key characteristics of a meaningful business goal. When business goals are aligned on the company, departmental, team, and individual levels, efforts are deliberately coordinated and focused on achieving results that are most important for the company's success.

In this example, the Marketing, Information Technology, and Production departments have goals that align with and support the company's goals. This alignment and support continue at all levels of the company.

For example, John's and Mary's goals align with the Help Desk team's goals, which align with Information Technology's goals, which align with the company's goals.

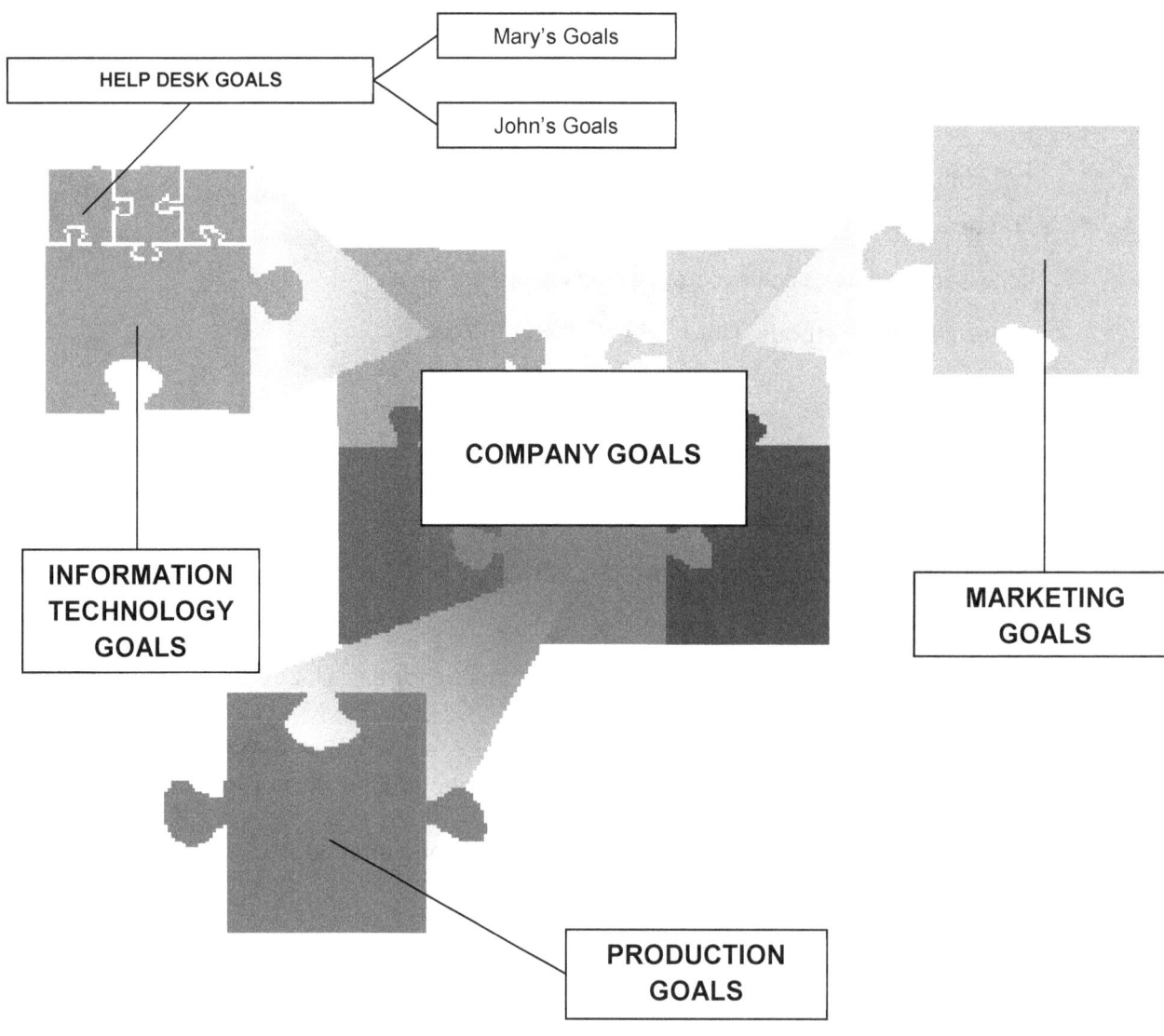

The Goal Alignment Cycle

Your company's strategy (or most important business goals if there is no formal strategy) should be the starting point for the creation of department, team, and individual goals. Company strategy leads to the creation of department goals that support it. Department goals lead to the creation of team and individual goals that support them. Once goals are set, individual team members begin performing to achieve them. Achievement of individual goals leads to achievement of team, department, and company results. This is an ongoing cycle that adjusts each performance year as company strategy (or most important goals) evolves.

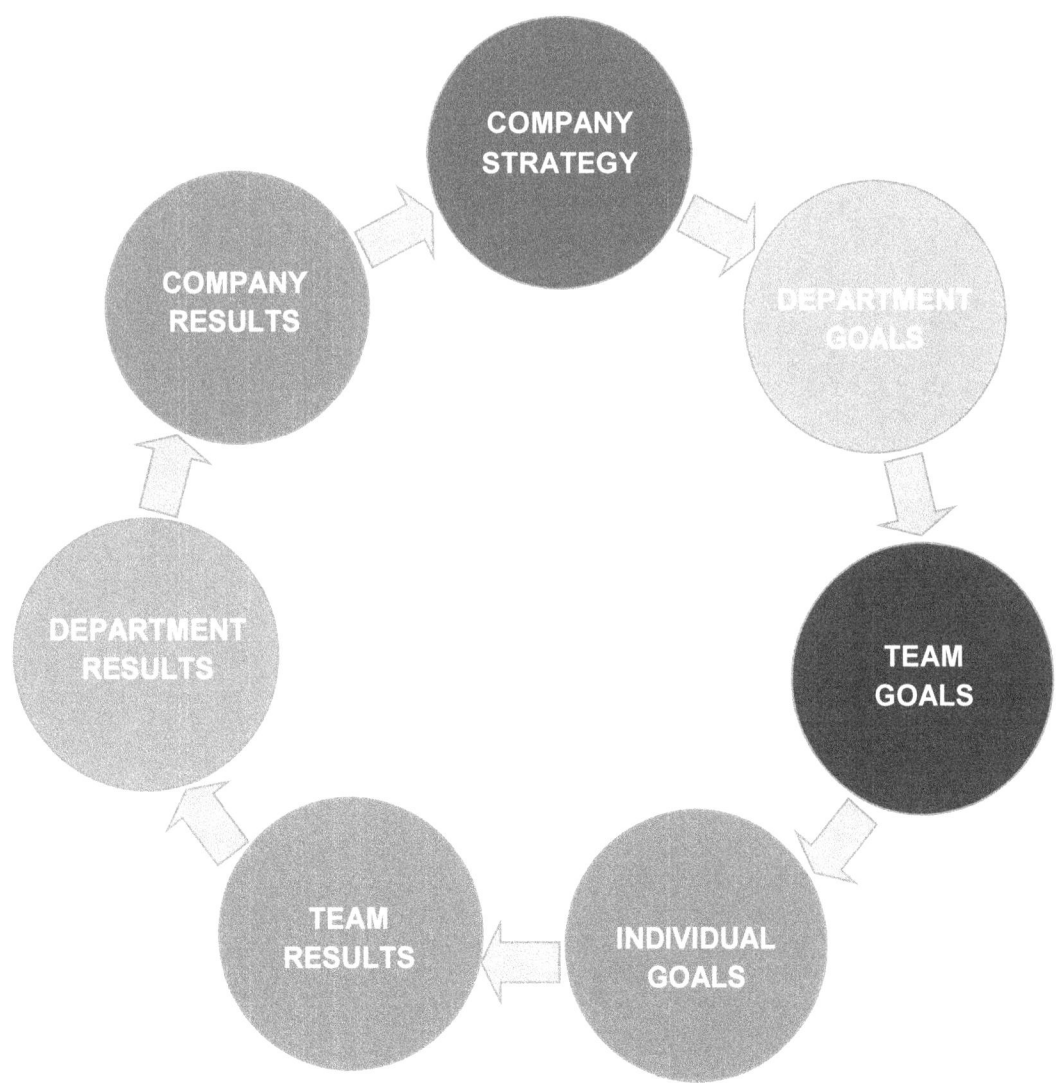

There are five steps to setting clear expectations for your team:

Step one: Align performance with organizational strategy

Step two: Write departmental goals

Step three: Write and delegate individual team member goals

Step four: Identify critical competencies

Step five: Communicate performance expectations

Use the Expectation Setting Worksheet on the following pages to think through and execute these steps.

Expectation Setting Worksheet

Managers with Direct Reports

Step One: Align Performance with Organizational Strategy

This is the step that has the greatest impact on your team's credibility and contribution to your company. Your department and team exist for a reason, right? Let's hope so. If not, your company would have eliminated them by now. During this step, take some time to think about and write down your team's purpose, reason for existing, and overall value to your company's achievement of its most important strategic goals.

Below are critical factors to consider as you think through your team's goals.

1. **What is the purpose of your team?**

_____
_____
_____
_____
_____
_____
_____
_____
_____
_____

2. **What are your team's key areas of responsibility?**

   Tip: A key area of responsibility is a critical output that requires your team's attention, manpower, and resources. Key areas of responsibility in many teams include the categories of operations, finance, and people.

_____
_____
_____
_____
_____
_____
_____
_____
_____
_____

3. **What are your company's most important business goals?**

_____
_____
_____
_____
_____
_____
_____
_____
_____
_____
_____
_____

4. **How can your team most appropriately support or impact your company's most important business goals?**

_____
_____
_____
_____
_____
_____
_____
_____
_____
_____
_____
_____

5. **What future forces are impacting your team's work?**

    Tip: _Most future forces fall into two categories:_

    A. _Internal factors such as staffing levels, senior leadership emphasis, and the company's financial outlook._

    B. _External factors, such as events at the local, regional, national, and global levels affecting the company, as well as competition, industry changes, new government regulations, and economic conditions._

_____
_____
_____
_____
_____
_____
_____
_____
_____
_____

6. **Given the opportunities you identified to support your company's business goals (item #3), along with the future forces impacting your team (item #4), list the business goals you believe will be important for your team to address in the coming year:**

_____
_____
_____
_____
_____
_____
_____
_____
_____
_____
_____
_____
_____
_____
_____
_____
_____
_____
_____
_____
_____
_____
_____

7. **List any team business goals still in progress that are likely to carry over from the current year to the coming year. Should any of these goals be modified based on the thought process you completed in steps 1–5? List modifications below.**

_____
_____
_____
_____
_____
_____
_____
_____
_____
_____
_____
_____
_____
_____
_____
_____
_____
_____
_____
_____
_____

8. **What other departments or teams will need to be involved to successfully complete your team business goals? What level of involvement will be needed from these departments or teams? What actions will be necessary to gain this involvement? How will the goal be impacted if the other departments or teams do not participate?**

_____
_____
_____
_____
_____
_____
_____
_____
_____
_____
_____
_____
_____
_____
_____
_____

Step Two: Write Department/Team Goals

9. **Compile a final draft of your annual team business goals based on the lists defined in items #6 and #7.**

> *__Tip:__ Use the worksheets on pages 11–24. Once the goals are written, take a second look at them. Ask yourself, "Given the priorities of my department, is there anything else that needs to be accomplished by my team in the coming year?" Adjust your team business goals as needed.*

> *__Tip:__ Goals should be SMART (Specific, Measurable, Achievable, Relevant, and Time-bound). Use the examples on pages 28–33 for guidance, if needed.*

Department Goal Worksheet (Example)

Department/Team Goal #1:

By 9/31/2017, launch a ten-week training program that develops fundamental management and leadership skills in newly promoted first-time managers and supervisors. Incorporate a blended learning approach that includes 50 percent instructor-led training, 50 percent self-paced online learning, and on-the-job application. Demonstrate a 20-percent increase in effectiveness ratings of managers who complete the program.

Due Date:
9/31/2017

Team Member(s) Responsible:

Sheila Davis
Robert Smith
Tom Nance

Team Member #1 Version of Goal Due: 8/15/2017	Competencies Required (Knowledge/Skills/Behaviors):
Sheila Davis *By 8/15/2017, research, develop, test, and finalize five instructor-led modules for the ten-week new-manager development program. Include modules focused on behavior-based interviewing, team building, goal setting, coaching, and change management. Achieve an overall quality rating of 90 percent from participants and their managers.*	*Instructional Design* *Project Management* *Leading Effective Meetings* *Collaboration* *Managing Work*
Team Member #2 Version of Goal **Due: 8/15/2017**	**Competencies Required** **(Knowledge/Skills/Behaviors):**
Robert Smith *By 8/15/2017, research, develop, test, and finalize five self-paced, online modules for the ten-week new-manager development program. Include modules focused on performance management, delegation, rewards and recognition, conflict management, and time management. Achieve an overall quality rating of 90 percent from participants and their managers.*	*Web-Based Instructional Design* *Project Management* *Leading Effective Meetings* *Collaboration* *Managing Work*
Team Member #3 Version of Goal **Due: 9/15/2017**	**Competencies Required** **(Knowledge/Skills/Behaviors):**
Tom Nance *By 9/15/2017, develop, test, and finalize a software-based system for collecting and analyzing data related to the performance of new managers. Ensure that system provides accurate pretraining and posttraining performance data on participants who complete the new-manager development program.*	*Software Design* *Project Management* *Leading Effective Meetings* *Collaboration* *Managing Work*

Department/Team Goal Worksheet

Department/Team Goal #1:	
Due Date:	
Team Member(s) Responsible:	
Team Member #1 Version of Goal **Due:**	**Competencies Required** **(Knowledge/Skills/Behaviors):**
Team Member #2 Version of Goal **Due:**	**Competencies Required** **(Knowledge/Skills/Behaviors):**
Team Member #3 Version of Goal **Due:**	**Competencies Required** **(Knowledge/Skills/Behaviors):**

Department/Team Goal Worksheet

Department/Team Goal #2:	
Due Date:	
Team Member(s) Responsible:	
Team Member #1 Version of Goal **Due:**	**Competencies Required** **(Knowledge/Skills/Behaviors):**
Team Member #2 Version of Goal **Due:**	**Competencies Required** **(Knowledge/Skills/Behaviors):**
Team Member #3 Version of Goal **Due:**	**Competencies Required** **(Knowledge/Skills/Behaviors):**

Department/Team Goal Worksheet

Department/Team Goal #3:	
Due Date:	
Team Member(s) Responsible:	
Team Member #1 Version of Goal Due:	Competencies Required (Knowledge/Skills/Behaviors):
Team Member #2 Version of Goal Due:	Competencies Required (Knowledge/Skills/Behaviors):
Team Member #3 Version of Goal Due:	Competencies Required (Knowledge/Skills/Behaviors):

Department/Team Goal Worksheet

Department/Team Goal #4:	
Due Date:	
Team Member(s) Responsible:	
Team Member #1 Version of Goal **Due:**	**Competencies Required** **(Knowledge/Skills/Behaviors):**
Team Member #2 Version of Goal **Due:**	**Competencies Required** **(Knowledge/Skills/Behaviors):**
Team Member #3 Version of Goal **Due:**	**Competencies Required** **(Knowledge/Skills/Behaviors):**

Department/Team Goal Worksheet

Department /Team Goal #5:	
Due Date:	
Team Member(s) Responsible:	
Team Member #1 Version of Goal **Due:**	**Competencies Required** **(Knowledge/Skills/Behaviors):**
Team Member #2 Version of Goal **Due:**	**Competencies Required** **(Knowledge/Skills/Behaviors):**
Team Member #3 Version of Goal **Due:**	**Competencies Required** **(Knowledge/Skills/Behaviors):**

Department/Team Goal Worksheet

Department/Team Goal #6:	
Due Date:	
Team Member(s) Responsible:	
Team Member #1 Version of Goal **Due:**	**Competencies Required** **(Knowledge/Skills/Behaviors):**
Team Member #2 Version of Goal **Due:**	**Competencies Required** **(Knowledge/Skills/Behaviors):**
Team Member #3 Version of Goal **Due:**	**Competencies Required** **(Knowledge/Skills/Behaviors):**

Department/Team Goal Worksheet

Department/Team Goal #7:	
Due Date:	
Team Member(s) Responsible:	
Team Member #1 Version of Goal **Due:**	**Competencies Required** **(Knowledge/Skills/Behaviors):**
Team Member #2 Version of Goal **Due:**	**Competencies Required** **(Knowledge/Skills/Behaviors):**
Team Member #3 Version of Goal **Due:**	**Competencies Required** **(Knowledge/Skills/Behaviors):**

Department/Team Goal Worksheet

Department/Team Goal #8:	
Due Date:	
Team Member(s) Responsible:	

Team Member #1 Version of Goal Due:	Competencies Required (Knowledge/Skills/Behaviors):
Team Member #2 Version of Goal Due:	Competencies Required (Knowledge/Skills/Behaviors):
Team Member #3 Version of Goal Due:	Competencies Required (Knowledge/Skills/Behaviors):

Department/Team Goal Worksheet

Department/Team Goal #9:	
Due Date:	
Team Member(s) Responsible:	
Team Member #1 Version of Goal **Due:**	**Competencies Required** **(Knowledge/Skills/Behaviors):**
Team Member #2 Version of Goal **Due:**	**Competencies Required** **(Knowledge/Skills/Behaviors):**
Team Member #3 Version of Goal **Due:**	**Competencies Required** **(Knowledge/Skills/Behaviors):**

Department/Team Goal Worksheet

Department/Team Goal #10:	
Due Date:	
Team Member(s) Responsible:	
Team Member #1 Version of Goal **Due:**	**Competencies Required** **(Knowledge/Skills/Behaviors):**
Team Member #2 Version of Goal **Due:**	**Competencies Required** **(Knowledge/Skills/Behaviors):**
Team Member #3 Version of Goal **Due:**	**Competencies Required** **(Knowledge/Skills/Behaviors):**

Department/Team Goal Worksheet

Department/Team Goal #11:	
Due Date:	
Team Member(s) Responsible:	
Team Member #1 Version of Goal **Due:**	**Competencies Required** **(Knowledge/Skills/Behaviors):**
Team Member #2 Version of Goal **Due:**	**Competencies Required** **(Knowledge/Skills/Behaviors):**
Team Member #3 Version of Goal **Due:**	**Competencies Required** **(Knowledge/Skills/Behaviors):**

Department/Team Goal Worksheet

Department/Team Goal #12:	
Due Date:	
Team Member(s) Responsible:	
Team Member #1 Version of Goal **Due:**	**Competencies Required** **(Knowledge/Skills/Behaviors):**
Team Member #2 Version of Goal **Due:**	**Competencies Required** **(Knowledge/Skills/Behaviors):**
Team Member #3 Version of Goal **Due:**	**Competencies Required** **(Knowledge/Skills/Behaviors):**

Department/Team Goal Worksheet

Department/Team Goal #13:	
Due Date:	
Team Member(s) Responsible:	
Team Member #1 Version of Goal **Due:**	**Competencies Required** **(Knowledge/Skills/Behaviors):**
Team Member #2 Version of Goal **Due:**	**Competencies Required** **(Knowledge/Skills/Behaviors):**
Team Member #3 Version of Goal **Due:**	**Competencies Required** **(Knowledge/Skills/Behaviors):**

Step Three: Write and Delegate Individual Team Member Goals

10. **Before assigning a member of your team to each business goal, consider the competencies required for successful goal achievement. Your company may have established competencies for certain roles. If not, consult a competency reference book. There are several on the market at reasonable prices. I recommend *For Your Improvement* by Michael M. Lonbardo.**

11. **Given the competencies essential for each business goal, identify who in your department is best suited for each goal.**

    Tip: You may find it helpful to divide goal assignments into "lead" and "support" roles to reinforce teamwork and create opportunities for professional development.

    As a manager, you are responsible for assigning work to your team members by matching projects to the most qualified person available.

    When thinking about assigning a project leader, consider past performance on similar projects and whether you want to use an assignment as an opportunity for a team member's professional development.

    If you have a team member with development needs, assigning the team member to a support role on a goal will provide an opportunity to learn new skills. This approach also helps prevent the team member from becoming overwhelmed.

12. **Estimate the expected completion dates for each of the business goals.**

13. **Use the worksheets on pages 12–24 to document your department/team and individual team member goals.**

Step Four: Identify Critical Competencies

Identify the four to six competencies essential for achievement of assigned business goals and successful overall job performance. Your organization may have already identified these competencies. If not, select them from a competency reference guide. There are several on the market that are reasonably priced. I recommend *For Your Improvement* by Michael M. Lombardo.

To make competency expectations clear to yourself and the team member, ensure that each competency has a name and a description that includes a list of observable actions that describe what it "looks like" when it is demonstrated effectively. This makes it easier to observe how effectively the team member is demonstrating each competency. For example:

Competency Name: *Building Trust*

Competency Definition: *Interacts with others in a way that gives them confidence in your intentions*

Observable Actions:

☐ *Operates with integrity—demonstrates honesty; keeps commitments; behaves in a consistent manner*

☐ *Discloses own positions—shares thoughts, feelings, and rationale so others understand personal positions*

☐ *Remains open to ideas—listens to others and objectively considers their ideas and opinions; supports others—treats people with dignity, respect, and fairness; gives proper credit to others; stands up for deserving others and their ideas even in the face of resistance or challenge*

☐ *Allows learning from mistakes—encourages new, innovative thinking*

Step Five: Communicate Performance Expectations

14. **Schedule a meeting with your upline manager to review and gain approval of the performance expectations you set and assigned. Revise as needed.**

15. **Schedule a meeting with each team member to communicate performance expectations, including each specific goal and competency for which the team member is responsible.**

    Tip: Encourage the team member to ask questions and provide input to enhance ownership and motivation.

    Tip: Ensure that each team member has easy access to his or her most current performance expectations throughout the performance year.

Performance Expectations: Final Check

Each team member's performance expectations should clearly communicate what success will look like for the team member at the end of the performance period. These expectations are expressed as goals (what the team member is expected to do) and competencies (how the team member is expected to do it). For example, a doctor might be expected to treat ten patients per day throughout the year (goal) and employ excellent bedside manner with each patient (competency).

- For each of your team members, ensure that performance expectations clearly communicate *what* results are to be achieved and *how* the team member is to go about achieving them.

- Ensure that that each team member has four to eight SMART goals that represent at least 90 percent of his or her job.

- Ensure that each team member has four to six competencies representing the knowledge, skills, and abilities necessary for achieving his or her goals. If your company does not have established competency models, use a competency resource such as *For Your Improvement* by Michael M. Lombardo as a source of prewritten competencies.

Goals + Competencies = Performance Expectations

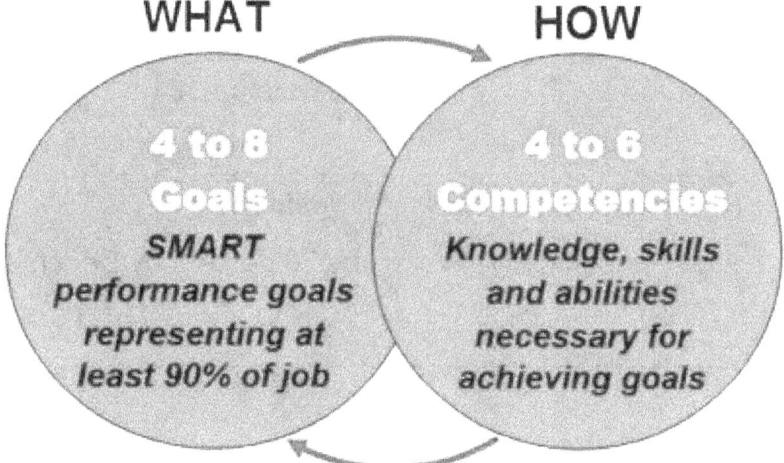

Goal Examples

Cascaded Goal

President

Increase company revenue by 20 percent by December 31, 2017.

Vice-President

Launch a new online learning business by August 31, 2017.

Director

Design and implement a strategy for developing and marketing ten core online learning products by March 31, 2017.

Manager

Ensure the design and delivery of ten comprehensive, highly engaging, online learning products by July 31, 2017. Ensure products align with Director's strategy and are interactive, engaging, and meet adult learning expectations.

Team Member

Design and deliver Business Strategy, SWOT Analysis, and Porter's Five Forces online learning courses by June 30, 2017.

Process Goal
Run and deliver the customer satisfaction report by 5:30 p.m. every Friday throughout 2017.

Outcome Goal
Redesign and relaunch the company's community outreach program by September 30, 2017.

Creative Goal
Write at least one magazine article per month that meets the established quality expectations for a "front-of-section" piece.

Simple Project Goal
Manage the project of configuring the new payroll system for the company. Implement the system throughout the organization, as appropriate, by October 1, 2017.

Detailed Project Goal

Manage the project of designing, developing, implementing, and evaluating a new intranet website for the company. Implement the new intranet website by October 1, 2017.

- **Subtasks**

  - Conduct best-practice research and external benchmarking using a variety of sources, both inside and outside the industry.

  - Meet with key team members at all levels of the organization to determine intranet website needs. Obtain feedback regarding recommendations for improving the current intranet website.

  - Design the new intranet website using data collected externally and internally. Create specific, practical tools to guide line managers and team members through using the new intranet website effectively.

  - Conduct due diligence and collect request for proposals from at least three vendors who specialize in designing corporate intranet websites.

  - Partner with Information Technology to determine feasibility of designing and building a comprehensive intranet website internally.

  - Decide which course of action (build internally or contract with a vendor) to pursue based on project scope and goals and execute the action steps.

  - Create a total communication strategy for the new intranet website, including timing and content for broadcast e-mails to all team members; information to senior leaders and managers; webinars and live demonstrations to team members; and so forth.

SMART Goals

SMART goals make it clear what will be accomplished, to what expectations, by when, and how success will be measured. Clear, specific goals that define what success will look like at appraisal time set team members up to succeed, make course correction easier during the performance period, and—when discussed frequently—eliminate unpleasant surprises at appraisal time.

SMART stands for:

Specific

Measurable

Achievable

Relevant

Time-bound

Example:

Reduce office supply expenses five percent by the end of the year by implementing an ongoing centralized office supply–ordering process that reduces waste and minimizes duplicate orders.

Specific: Reduce office supply expenses five percent by the end of the year by implementing an ongoing centralized office supply–ordering process that reduces waste and minimizes duplicate orders.

Measurable: Reduce office expenses five percent.

Achievable: This is possible to achieve.

Relevant: Saving money is relevant to the company's financial bottom line.

Time-bound: This goal has a deadline of by year-end.

Identifying SMART Goals

To ensure that performance is clearly defined for the manager and the team member, goals must be SMART. Anything less will eventually lead to misunderstanding and less-than-desired performance results. Test your ability to identify SMART goals with the exercise below. The answers are on the next page.

Goal	Is This Goal SMART? Why or Why Not?
1) Improve internal customer service at the IT Help Desk by the end of the third quarter.	
2) Increase prime-time advertising sales by three percent by June 30, 2017.	
3) Implement a loyalty program marketing strategy with TV, radio, and print components, which will sign up forty thousand members.	
4) Launch the SAP system across the organization by December 31, 2017.	
5) Significantly improve the quality of our product by the end of the third quarter, 2017.	
6) Answer at least 90 percent of incoming calls within three rings with a friendly, professional greeting throughout 2017.	
7) By the end of the third quarter, reduce from three days to two days the amount of time it takes to produce monthly reports.	

Identifying SMART Goals (Answers)

Goal	Is This Goal SMART? Why or Why Not?
1) Improve internal customer service at the IT Help Desk by the end of the third quarter.	*No. This goal is not specific. Improve which aspects of customer service? It is also not measurable. Improve to what level?*
2) Increase prime-time advertising sales by three percent by June 30, 2017.	*Yes. This goal is specific, measurable, achievable, relevant, and time-bound.*
3) Implement a loyalty program marketing strategy with TV, radio, and print components, which will sign up forty thousand members.	*No. This goal is not time-bound. It has no deadline. By when is this goal expected to be achieved?*
4) Launch the SAP system across the organization by December 31, 2017.	*Yes. This goal is specific, measurable, achievable, relevant, and time-bound.*
5) Significantly improve the quality of our product by the end of the third quarter, 2017.	*No. This goal is not specific. Improve which aspects of product quality? It is also not measurable. Which aspects of product quality will be measured? What specific targets do we want to achieve?*
6) Answer at least 90 percent of incoming calls within three rings with a friendly, professional greeting throughout 2017.	*Yes. This goal is specific, measurable, achievable, relevant, and time-bound.*
7) By the end of the third quarter, reduce from three days to two days the amount of time it takes to produce monthly reports.	*Yes. This goal is specific, measurable, achievable, relevant, and time-bound.*

Phase One: Set Expectations—Key Points

1. Identify your organization's business strategy and most important business goals for the year.

2. If you are a manager, write four to eight SMART business goals for your department/team to achieve during the year. Ensure that these goals support (directly or indirectly) your company's most important business goals. These goals become your annual goals as the manager.

3. Discuss your goals with your manager. Adjust as needed and gain your manager's approval of your goals.

4. Communicate your team/department goals to your direct reports.

5. Write four to eight SMART business goals for each of your direct reports. These goals should support your department/team goals and should represent at least 90 percent of the direct report's job.

6. If your organization does not already have competencies (key knowledge, skills, and behaviors) identified for team members, select four to six competencies for each team member. For fairness and consistency, it's best to assign the same competencies to team members who do the same job. Refer to a competency reference book such as *For Your Improvement* by Michael M. Lombardo for additional guidance.

7. Conduct a one-on-one meeting with each direct report to review company goals, department/team goals, and his or her individual goals. Explain how his or her individual goals support the department/team goals and the company's goals. Review competencies and explain that they define the knowledge, skills, and behaviors needed to achieve individual goals. Request team member input on individual goals and make adjustments as appropriate.

8. Enter team goals, direct reports' goals, and direct reports' competencies into your organization's performance management system (if you have one) or into a shared document that you and your direct reports can access anytime for reference, tracking, and status updates.

Phase Two: Review Progress

Desired Outcomes

- Regular progress meetings (at least monthly) scheduled and conducted with each direct report

- Coaching provided to each direct report, as needed, to maximize opportunities for successful performance

- Informal, real-time feedback given to each direct report as needed

- Performance notes kept for each direct report throughout the performance year

A manager recently said to me, "I set expectations for one of my team members. She did not meet those expectations during the year, and I noted that on her performance appraisal. Boy, was she upset! She thought she was doing a better job than I thought she was doing. She was surprised by how I rated her on her appraisal."

The takeaway here is that effective performance requires more than just setting and communicating expectations at the beginning of the performance year. This "set it and forget it" approach almost always results in unpleasant surprises at appraisal time, when the manager and the team member realize that they have different ideas about how well the team member performed. This situation is one of the main reasons managers and team members dread performance appraisals.

Remember the road trip analogy we used in the Set Expectations section of this book? Well, not reviewing team members' progress toward established expectations is like setting out on a road trip and not checking—on a regular basis—to make sure you are on the right road and progressing on schedule. At the end of the trip, you are likely to discover that you are in the wrong city, behind schedule, and over budget.

To stay on track during a road trip, you would do things such as the following:

- Check to see if you are covering enough distance each hour or day
- Refer to a map, GPS system, and road signs to ensure that you remain on course
- Make sure you are staying within budget on fuel, food, and so forth
- Give feedback to the driver, navigator, and others about how they are performing toward the expectations you set
- Coach the driver, navigator, and others as needed if they need to change their performance to ensure that expectations are met by the end of the trip

I recently had a conversation with a manager about this:

Manager: I have a team member who is really upset about the performance appraisal I gave her.

Me: Why is she upset?

Manager: She disagrees with the ratings I gave her and with the comments I made. She really didn't meet the expectations I set.

Me: But she thinks she did?

Manager: Yes. She's really surprised by this. I don't get why. Her goals and competencies are in the performance management system where she can see them.

Me: How often did you meet with her during the year to give her feedback and coach her toward the performance you expected?

Manager: I let her know if she dropped the ball on something. I don't do regular meetings with my team members because I don't have the time.

Me: You might want to consider scheduling regular meetings with each team member—weekly, semiweekly, or at least monthly. Thirty minutes is usually enough, but schedule an hour in case you need it. Put all of the meetings on your calendar at the beginning of the year before your calendar fills up. That'll give you enough check-in opportunities to give specific feedback and to coach your team member back on track if she is veering off. You and you team member will avoid those unpleasant surprises next year at appraisal time.

Manager: What do I do now?

Me: If you need my help discussing it with the team member, let's schedule a meeting. Your best bet going forward is to put a plan in place for regularly reviewing progress toward expectations next year.

Reviewing Progress: Some Additional Wisdom

When an airplane takes off it has a flight plan. However, during the course of the flight, wind, rain, turbulence, air traffic, human error, and other factors keep knocking the plane off course. In fact, a plane is off course about 90 percent of the time. The key is that the pilots keep making small course corrections by reading their instruments and talking to the control tower. As a result, a plane reaches its destination.

—Sean Covey

A little progress every day adds up to big results.

—Satya Nani

Some of our poor choices are irreversible, but many are not. Often, we can change course and get back on the right track.

—James E. Faust

There are four steps to setting clear expectations for your team:

Step one: Create a performance notes system

Step two: Schedule a year's worth of one-on-one meetings

Step three: Provide ongoing feedback and coaching

Step four: Discuss and document performance regularly

Let's take a closer look at these steps and how to execute them.

Step One: Create a Performance Notes System

A performance notes system is essential for a number of reasons. It enables you to document your team members' performance as objectively as possible in a manner that focuses on observable, job-related behaviors. At appraisal time, having notes that accurately document how each team member performed toward expectations throughout the entire performance year makes it easier to write a fair and accurate appraisal. It also makes it easier to avoid "recency bias" in which a manager bases the appraisal mostly on a team member's performance during the last few months of the year, which is easiest to recall.

There are many ways to create a performance notes system. Your company may have a performance notes feature built into its performance management software. If not, you can create a simple and easy to use system using e-mail folders, word processing software such as Microsoft Word, or spreadsheet software such as Microsoft Excel. Of these three options, I recommend creating an Excel spreadsheet, which will make it easier to sort and retrieve your notes on each team member at appraisal time.

Regardless of the method you choose, make sure your performance notes system allows you to log notes that include the team member's name, what the note is about, the date, and the note itself. You might also want to include the goal or competency to which the note applies. Here's an example:

Team Member	Subject	Date	Note
Frieda Livery	Missed Deadline	8/17/2017	*Frieda missed the deadline on completing the facilitator's guide for the revised New Employee Orientation program. The facilitator's guide was due today to keep the instructor training session on schedule. I discussed this with Frieda and emphasized the necessity of meeting milestones and deadlines on her projects. I asked her for ideas on how to get back on schedule. She agreed to finish the facilitator's guide tonight so that it will be ready in time for the instructor training session on August 22. I emphasized the importance of meeting deadlines, and Frieda stated that it would not happen again.*

Step Two: Schedule a Year's Worth of One-on-One Meetings

Yes, I know. You're probably thinking, *How on earth can I schedule one-on-one meetings with my entire team for an entire year? I don't have time for that.* My advice is to make time. Ensuring that you are checking in with your team members regularly enough to keep them performing on track is the most effective way to achieve successful individual and team performance. If you wait too long to check progress, give feedback, and provide coaching, you are likely to end up with results that do not meet expectations—and it will be too late to course correct before the performance period ends.

Scheduling one-on-one meetings for your team members is simple, so I won't go into a lot of detail here. Just make sure that at the beginning of the performance year you do the following:

- Schedule meetings with each direct report for the entire year. Meetings should be weekly, every other week, or, at a minimum, monthly Schedule the meetings with each team member on the same day of the week or month and at the same time. This will create a cadence and help make the regular meetings a habit.

- Schedule at least thirty minutes for each meeting. (I schedule an hour, in case more time is needed, but the meetings usually take thirty minutes.)

- Put the recurring meetings on your electronic calendar. (I recommend using the one attached to your company's e-mail system.)

- Make sure the meeting invitations are on the team member's electronic calendar as well.

I guarantee that you will need to reschedule some of these meetings throughout the year. That's to be expected, and it's OK. If you need to cancel a meeting, however, reschedule it for the next available time slot of have a brief, less formal check-in with the team member via phone or e-mail.

Step Three: Provide Ongoing Feedback and Coaching

Providing ongoing feedback and coaching gives you the opportunity to praise good performance and encourage it to continue. It also enables you to keep track of performance toward expectations, identify performance that is veering off course, and course correct early enough to ensure successful performance by the end of the performance period. Conceptually, this is the same approach that keeps airliners on course toward their destinations. Commercial airliners are off course 90 percent of the time they are in flight. Constant reading of gauges and indicators and communication with air traffic controllers give pilots the information they need to continuously course correct and reach their intended destinations.

Providing feedback isn't always easy, especially when it's corrective feedback. It is, however, an essential part of a manager's job and is critical for ensuring effective team performance and achievement of goals. When giving feedback, remember the following:

- When you see it, say it. Provide feedback as soon as possible after observing the performance or behavior.
- Give positive feedback publicly, when possible. Give corrective feedback privately.
- Keep the feedback balanced. Do not provide only corrective feedback. Provide positive feedback as well when it is warranted. This will help prevent your team members from feeling like they are going to the principal's office every time you give them feedback.
- When delivering corrective feedback, remain calm and professional. Give the feedback with the intention of helping your team member to succeed. When the team member succeeds, you succeed.

The diagram on the next page provides a simple and effective approach for delivering positive and corrective feedback.

Giving Positive and Corrective Feedback

Positive Feedback Model*

Example: *"At today's staff meeting, I noticed that you contributed a lot of good ideas for reducing costs within the department. As a result, we'll have a far more robust list of recommendations to present to our VP at the next department meeting."*

Corrective Feedback Model*

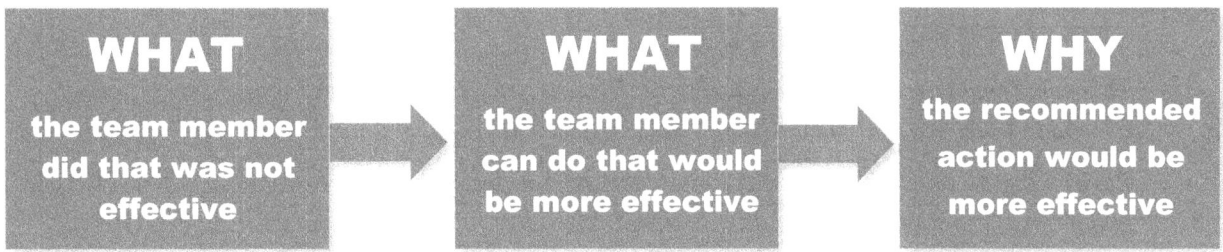

Example: *"I noticed that you have been late for work twice this week. As a result, we have been short staffed two mornings in a row, and on those mornings our customers did not receive their reports on time. It would be more effective for you to arrive on time every day. That will help ensure that we have the staffing we need to deliver reports to our customers on time."*

*Give positive feedback publicly, if possible. Give corrective feedback privately.

Coaching Overview

Coaching is an essential but often neglected part of a manager's job. When done effectively, it provides a means for keeping team members on track toward meeting or exceeding expectations. When done poorly or not done at all, it sets the stage for misunderstanding between the manager and team members, results that do not meet expectations, and lower team member engagement.

Coaching does not always need to be formal. Short informal coaching discussions on a regular basis, like the autopilot on a commercial aircraft, are the most effective way to keep team members on course for successful performance. Formal discussions also have their place, particularly when significant course correction is needed to put a team member on the path to successful performance.

The biggest mistake managers make in regard to coaching is to think of it primarily as a corrective or punitive action against a team member. Although this can be the case if the situation warrants, it is far more effective to think of coaching as a tool to position team members for success. Think about it. World-class athletes, Olympic medalists, and championship sports teams have coaches. Why do they need coaches if they are already at the top of their respective games? To continue performing effectively and to take their performance to even higher levels—that's why. When applied to a work team, this approach benefits not only the individual team member, but the manager as well when the team member achieves results.

Types of Coaching

There are three types of coaching: positioning for success, positioning for improvement, and managing performance issues.

Positioning for success involves coaching a team member or an entire team taking on a new task, assignment, project, or responsibility in which they have little to no experience. In this type of coaching, the manager focuses the discussion on

- explaining the new task, assignment, project, or responsibility;
- defining the ideal outcome (what success will look like);
- identifying the knowledge and skills the team member will need to develop and apply to be successful;
- identifying the support and resources the team member will need to be successful; and
- agreeing on how progress will be reviewed and monitored.

Positioning for improvement involves coaching a team member or an entire team whose performance is beginning to veer off track. Although performance may be below expectations, the idea is to course correct and coach toward a successful outcome. In this type of coaching, the manager focuses the discussion on

- communicating the performance or behavior that was observed;
- providing specific examples of this performance or behavior;

- gaining the team member's (or team's) perspective on the situation;
- clarifying the task, assignment, project, or responsibility;
- clarifying the ideal outcome (what success will look like);
- asking for the team member's (or team's) ideas on how to improve the performance or behavior;
- identifying the support and resources needed to get back on the path to success (without removing the team member's or team's responsibility); and
- agreeing on how progress will be reviewed and monitored.

Managing performance issues involves coaching a team member whose performance has continuously been below expectations or who had demonstrated serious misconduct. Coaching to manage a performance issue should be done when repeated coaching has not resulted in improved performance. In this type of coaching, the manager focuses the discussion on

- communicating the performance or behavior that was observed;
- providing specific examples of this performance or behavior;
- reviewing expectations and agreements set during previous coaching conversations;
- clearly explaining the consequences if the performance does not improve within a specified period of time (no more than thirty days); and
- agreeing on how progress will be reviewed and monitored.

Coaching Conversation Planner

Positioning for success is typically the easiest of the coaching conversations. In this situation, the individual or team being coached has not yet begun the new assignment. The likelihood of defensiveness—and its accompanying emotions—becoming part of the discussion is low.

Positioning for improvement and managing performance issues are usually more difficult conversations for the manager and the team member. No one enjoys hearing that his or her performance is below expectations, and defensiveness, anger, and other emotions typically erupt during these conversations, making it difficult for the manager to keep the discussion on track.

To manage these coaching conversations in a way that treats the team member with respect, defuses strong emotions, and, when appropriate, refocuses the team member on successful performance, use the coaching conversation planner on the following pages to plan the discussion in advance. Use it as a road map during the conversation, too, to remain focused and on track.

The five steps of the coaching conversation are

1. begin the conversation,
2. define the situation,
3. explore ideas for success,
4. confirm the plan for success, and
5. conclude the conversation.

These steps are detailed on the pages that follow.

Coaching Conversation Planner

Use this conversation planner to prepare your coaching discussion in advance. Use the planner as a road map during your conversation and add additional notes as needed.

Person or Team: **Date:**

Before the Conversation

What's the Context?

What situation or task needs to be discussed?
(Is the person or team taking on a new task or responsibility? Is performance off track on an existing task or responsibility?)

Why is this situation or task important?
(What can be gained if success is achieved? What is at stake if success is not achieved?)

What is the ideal outcome of discussing this situation or task?
(What should be understood, clarified, or achieved at the conclusion of this discussion?)

What opportunities are present within this situation or task?
(How can the person/team/department/company benefit from the successful completion of this situation or task?)

What challenges are present in this situation or task?
(What might the individual/team/department/company need to learn or overcome while managing this situation/task?)

What does success in this situation or task look like? What results should be achieved?
(Paint a clear picture of the successful outcome.)

How will success be measured?
(Include outcomes, metrics, deadlines, etc.)

What's the Plan for Managing Reactions?

How is this person or team likely to react to this discussion?

What will I do during the discussion to manage these reactions and keep the person/team open to communicating?

☐ *Show Empathy*

- Acknowledge the person's/team's feelings (not necessary to agree with feelings).

☐ *Maintain Self-Respect*

- Focus on specific, observed behavior, not the person or team personally.
- Give genuine, positive feedback when appropriate.

☐ *Encourage Involvement*

- Ask questions to inspire ideas.
- Ask and listen 80 percent of the time; share and tell 20 percent of the time.

☐ *Be Open about Thoughts and Feelings*

- Share thoughts and feelings about the situation appropriately to build trust.

☐ *Provide Support and Resources*

- Guide the person/team toward success while holding him/her/them accountable for results.

During the Conversation

How Will I Manage Each Phase of the Conversation?

(State the reason for the conversation. What is the specific situation or task that needs to be discussed?)

Begin *the conversation*

(Ask questions and share observations to clarify the situation for yourself and the person/team; gather, share, and confirm facts.)

Questions and Observations:

Define *the situation*

(Ask questions to draw out and discuss ideas for successful performance.)

Questions and Observations:

Explore
ideas for
success

What specific actions will be taken by the person/team? What backup plans are needed? How will progress be measured?

If managing a chronic performance issue that has been repeatedly discussed, by when must performance be improved? What will the consequences be if improved performance is not achieved?

Actions/Backup Plan/Progress Measurement Plan:

Confirm *the*
plan for
success

(Recap the key points of the plan, verify commitment from the person/team, and restate your commitment to provide support and resources needed for success.)

Conclude *the conversation*

After the Conversation

What Agreements Were Made?

Action/By When	Person Responsible

How Will Progress Be Reviewed?

(Weekly/daily check-in meetings, weekly/daily reports, observation and feedback by manager, meeting interim targets, etc.)

How Will Results Be Measured?

(What specific targets will be met? What specific results will be achieved? By when?)

How Did the Conversation Go?

What went well?

What, if anything, did not go well?

What will I do differently next time?

Step Four: Discuss and Document Performance Regularly

Now that you have a performance notes system, one-on-one progress meetings scheduled, and methods for providing coaching and feedback, all that's left to do is to follow through with the systems you have put in place. Meet with each team member as scheduled. Reschedule as soon as possible if you cannot attend a meeting. Have informal, ad hoc check-ins with your team members between scheduled meetings when necessary. Document notable performance (positive or corrective) in your performance notes system so you will have the information you need to write accurate appraisals at the end of the performance period. Follow through with these actions and you will eliminate unpleasant surprises for you and your team members at appraisal time.

Phase Two: Review Progress—Key Points

1. Set performance expectations (goals and competencies) within the first thirty days of the performance year.

2. At the beginning of the performance year, schedule one-on-one meetings with each team member for the entire year (schedule meetings for at least thirty minutes and conduct them weekly, semiweekly, or monthly).

3. Use your one-on-one meetings to discuss progress toward established performance expectations (goals and competencies), provide positive or corrective feedback, and provide coaching to position for success, position for improvement, or manage performance issues.

4. When you see it, say it; provide positive or corrective feedback as soon as possible after the observed performance or behavior.

5. Keep performance notes throughout the year on each of your team members; document feedback given, feedback received from others, coaching conversations, and anything that should be included on the year-end appraisal.

6. Adjust performance expectations as needed throughout the year if there are legitimate reasons to do so (e.g., business needs have changed, a project was canceled, a deadline needs to be extended for reasons beyond the team member's control, etc.).

Phase Three: Appraise Performance

Desired Outcomes

- Fair, accurate appraisal of team members' performance toward expectations (goals and competencies) set and tracked during the performance year

- Team member self-appraisal to provide additional perspective and promote a sense of fairness and involvement

- Accurate performance ratings that differentiate performance that is below expectations, meets expectations, and exceeds expectations

- No surprises to the team member during the appraisal meeting

A director at my company, who had been very resistant to the performance management process, called me one day in the midst of our annual performance appraisal period. The conversation went something like this:

Manager: Peter, I just want to tell you that I've changed my tune. I didn't think it was necessary to set performance expectations and review progress toward them during the year. I especially didn't think it was worth the time to keep performance notes. To be honest, I did it because you required it.

Me: No worries, I hear that a lot.

Manager: Now that I am writing my team's appraisals, I see how all of these elements fit together. Yeah, I put in a lot of time tracking goals and keeping performance notes during the year, but it's making it much easier to write these appraisals. Before, I just gave my opinion on how I felt the team member was doing performance-wise. Now, I have specific things to appraise, and my appraisals are based on actual performance data I collected during the year.

Me: Great. How is your team responding to this?

Manager: It's made the appraisal meetings easier, especially the difficult ones. I have a team member who gets upset during her appraisal meeting and argues over her ratings. This year things were different. We had discussed how she was doing against expectations throughout the year, so there were no surprises. I still had to rate her below expectations in some areas, but I had the performance data to back it up, and she didn't argue with it. What a difference. I've gone from being the biggest skeptic of this process to the biggest supporter.

Writing accurate appraisals that reflect actual performance is far easier when you have taken the time to set and communicate expectations, review and document progress toward them throughout the year, and provide ongoing feedback and coaching as needed. This approach gives you the data you need to make fair and legally defensible decisions on promotions, compensation, terminations, and other performance-related topics.

Appraising Performance: Some Additional Wisdom

Put it before them briefly so they will read it, clearly so they will appreciate it, picturesquely so they will remember it and, above all, accurately so they will be guided by its light.

—Joseph Pulitzer

Accuracy of statement is one of the first elements of truth; inaccuracy is a near kin to falsehood.

—Tryon Edwards

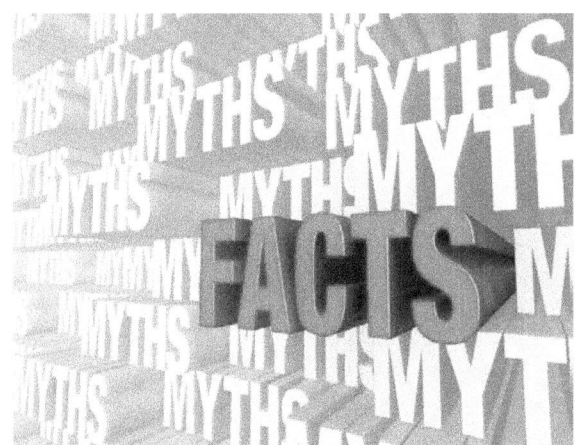

And in the absence of facts, myth rushes in, the kudzu of history.

—Stacy Schiff

There are five steps to writing a fair and accurate performance appraisal:
- – Step one: Review established expectations
- – Step two: Review performance toward established expectations
- – Step three: Write a fair and accurate performance appraisal
- – Step four: Prepare for the appraisal meeting
- – Step five: Conduct the appraisal meeting

Let's take a closer look at these steps and how to execute them.

Step One: Review Established Expectations

Begin by reviewing the expectations (goals and competencies) that you set for the team member at the beginning of the performance period. If you have been following the process, you have reviewed progress, provided feedback, coached, and documented performance on these expectations on a regular basis throughout the performance. As a result, these expectations should be up to date, but take a final look at them to ensure that any changes that have already been discussed with the team member have been made. This is not the time, however, to add new expectations that have not been communicated to the team member. That would be the equivalent of changing the rules of a race at the finish line and will result in unpleasant (and unfair) surprises for the team member during your appraisal meeting.

Here is an example of performance expectations for Pat Smith, a fictitious senior technical support team member:

Goals

1. During the first quarter (January 1 through March 31), receive average rating of 4.0 or above on all customer satisfaction measures

2. Improve average rating to 4.2 in second quarter (April 1 through June 30) and maintain this rating each quarter through December 31, 2017

3. Receive no more than two customer complaints per quarter

4. Complete plan for cross-training technical support team by March 31, 2017

5. Cross-train all technical support team members by May 31, 2017, achieving an overall training quality score of 90 percent

Competencies

1. *Developing Collaborative Relationships:* Develops and uses collaborative relationships to facilitate accomplishment of work goals between one's area and other areas, and departments to help achieve company business goals.

2. *Building Trust:* Interacts with others in a way that gives them confidence in one's intentions and those of the organization.

3. *Getting Results:* Demonstrates accountability for accomplishing objectives; performs successfully on a consistent basis; pushes for results; is bottom-line oriented.

4. *Customer Orientation*: Ensures that customers and their needs are a primary focus of one's actions; develops and maintains productive relationships with customers.

Step Two: Review Performance toward Established Expectations

After reviewing established performance expectations and ensuring that they are up to date, gather the data you collected throughout the year on the team member's performance toward these expectations. Include performance notes you kept, feedback you gave, feedback you received about the team member, and coaching conversations you documented. In addition, consider these other potential sources of performance data as appropriate:

- sales figures
- call records
- productivity reports
- deadline reports
- output and production records
- budget reports
- attendance records
- training or continuing education records
- customer compliments and complaints
- disciplinary notices

The main objective here is to gather all of the performance data you have collected for this specific team member throughout the performance year. This will prepare you to write a fair and accurate appraisal that reflects the team member's actual performance toward established expectations. Here is an example of performance data collected during the year for Pat Smith, a fictitious senior technical support team member:

- **February 1, 2017:** Pat completed the plan for team cross-training on February 1 (fourteen days ahead of schedule).

- **April 3, 2017:** Pat achieved a 3.6 average customer satisfaction rating during the first quarter, which was challenging considering her workload and the team's inexperience, but still within her control to achieve. I discussed this with Pat, and we identified areas in which she lost focus. We devised a plan to get this goal back on track.

- **June 1, 2017:** Pat got the team trained to handle technical questions from customers. She took the initiative to design, develop, and facilitate the training. The team said they found the training helpful. Pat also oversaw the task of updating the customer support website.

- **July 5, 2017:** Pat achieved a 3.8 average customer satisfaction rating. Her workload got heavier during this period because we had fewer people on the team than we had during the first quarter. Pat was the only one left who could answer technical questions. She got positive comments on technical skills from Mr. Lambert, an external customer. I thanked Pat but reiterated that the expectation was a 4.0 rating, which was still achievable for her during this period. We brainstormed ideas and a plan to achieve the goal during the next quarter.

- **September 12, 2017:** Today, I observed Pat building a positive relationship with a difficult customer, Charlie Evers. Charlie called me to compliment Pat's customer service skills.

- **November 15, 2017:** In November, Charlie Evers, a challenging, high-profile customer, complimented Pat for consistently going above and beyond to resolve issues and provide high levels of service.

- **December 1, 2017:** Pat got three complaints during the first quarter and three during the second quarter. She got one during the third quarter and one during the fourth quarter.

- **December 15, 2017:** I received eleven e-mails during the year complimenting Pat on her people skills, particularly her ability to listen to other people's ideas and collaborate to achieve goals.

Step Three: Write a Fair and Accurate Performance Appraisal

After reviewing established performance expectations and gathering specific data on the team member's performance toward these expectations, you are now ready to write the performance appraisal. When writing the appraisal, I highly recommend following the time-tested practices below:

- Insert the specific performance expectations (goals and competencies) into the appraisal form so they can each be rated individually. The appraisal template on pages 65–72 demonstrates how to include goals and competencies. An editable version is available for download at www.peakehumancapital.com.

- Send the appraisal form to the team member for a self-appraisal before you write your appraisal. This step seems counterintuitive to some managers, but it promotes a sense of involvement and fairness for the team member and usually provides additional information that makes the appraisal easier for the manager to write. Most team members welcome the opportunity to complete a self-appraisal, but some do not, so make the self-appraisal optional if that works best for your team. The appraisal template on pages 65–72 provides an example of how to include an employee self-appraisal. It is available for download at www.peakehumancapital.com.

- Rate the team member on each of the established goals and competencies using a rating scale that differentiates between performance that is below expectations, meets expectations, or exceeds expectations.

- Make it clear to the team member that a "meets expectations" rating means that 100 percent of the expectation was met, which is very good performance.

- Give an "exceeds expectations" rating only if the team member did more than what was specified in the established goal or competency.

- For example: If a team member's goal was to do A, B, and C by the end of the year, and the team member did A, B, C, *and* D, an "exceeds expectations" rating would be justified. If the team member did A, B, and C as expected, a "meets expectations" rating would be justified. If the team member did only A and B, a "below expectations" rating would be justified if there were no legitimate circumstances preventing the team member from achieving the goal. The rating scale example on page 61 provides additional information.

  - If the team member did A, B, and C by the end of the year as expected, a "meets expectations" rating would be justified *even if the team member worked extremely hard to achieve the goal.* In this case, an "exceeds expectations" would be justified on the competencies related to working hard (e.g., "Tenacity").

- Use performance data you collected throughout the year to provide comments that justify your ratings. Ensure team members who opt to complete a self-appraisal do the same. This helps team members understand the rating scale and helps reduce their resistance to the ratings their managers provide.

- Consider these questions when rating each goal and competency:

  - Did the team member meet, exceed, or fall below this goal or competency as written?

  - What specific performance data do I have to back this up?

  - What was the impact on the team, department, and/or company?

  - Were there factors outside of the team member's control that contributed to expectations not being met? If so, what were they?

  - What can the team member do to enhance performance during the next year?

  - What more can I and/or the company do to support the team member?

- Check the appraisal to ensure that you avoid common rating errors. The rating errors information on page 62 provides guidance.

The Rating Scale

This is the rating scale I have used successfully for the past decade. Whichever scale you use, be sure it clearly differentiates between performance that is below expectations, meets expectations, or exceeds expectations.

5 = Far exceeds expectations (150 percent of goal)*

4 = Exceeds expectations (110 percent of goal)*

3 = Meets expectations (100 percent of goal)*

2 = Below expectations (90 percent of goal)*

1 = Far below expectations (40 percent or less of goal)*

- This is not the same as the "A, B, C, D, F" grading scale used in schools.

- A "3" means the team member achieved 100 percent of the goal or competency and is a very good rating. It does not equal a "C," "70 percent," or mediocre performance.

Quantitative	**Qualitative**

Justify your ratings with quantitative data *(sales figures, deadlines met, etc.)* and/or qualitative data *(behavioral observations, reaction from customers and coworkers, etc.).*

For example, if you were judging a swim meet, you would evaluate performance quantitatively based on the time it took to complete the event. If you were judging gymnastics, you would understand the components of excellent performance and, within that framework, judge more qualitatively.

*Percentages are for illustrative purposes and are not intended to be exact.

Common Rating Errors

Using a sound rating scale and providing accurate performance data to justify your ratings will help you avoid these common rating errors:

- **Central tendency:** The tendency to ignore individual performance differences and rate all team members the same

- **Stereotyping:** Basing appraisals on fixed perceptions of performance instead of on actual performance

- **Opportunity bias:** The tendency to rate a team member higher or lower than warranted because of outside circumstances

- **Recency effect:** The tendency to rate a team member higher than warranted based on outstanding work performed immediately before the appraisal was written

- **Halo effect:** The tendency of a manager to overrate a favored team member

- **Leniency bias:** Giving the team member the benefit of the doubt, exaggerating positives and eliminating negatives

- **Horns effect:** The tendency to rate a team member lower than actual performance warrants

Tips for Avoiding Rating Errors

- Be aware of your feelings, opinions, and biases.

- Focus on the team member's actual performance toward established performance goals and competencies.

- Back up your ratings with behavioral evidence.

Rating Errors Checklist

After you have drawn conclusions about a team member's performance, ask yourself the following questions. If you answer "yes" to any of them, you have made rating errors that should be corrected.

- ☐ Have I rated the team member more highly than actual performance toward expectations warrants?

- ☐ Did I unfairly blame the team member for events out of his/her control?

- ☐ Did I allow personal biases to overshadow the team member's actual performance toward established expectations?

- ☐ Did I allow one aspect of the team member's performance to overshadow the other aspects?

- ☐ Did I rate the team member more highly because he/she and I are similar?

- ☐ Did I rate the team member lower because he/she and I are different?

- ☐ Did I rate the team member toward the middle of the scale to make the appraisal easier on myself?

- ☐ Did I exclude any of the team member's exceptionally good or exceptionally bad performance?

- ☐ Did I place too much emphasis on recent events and not enough on the entire year's performance?

- ☐ Have I made assumptions about or stereotyped the team member?

- ☐ Have I allowed fear of how the team member will react to impact the accuracy of my ratings and comments?

Avoiding Legal Trouble

As you put the finishing touches on a performance appraisal, review the following statements. If you cannot say any of them with certainty, then you may have stepped into a legal trap.

In this performance evaluation

☐ I did not make predictions about the team member's future opportunities.

☐ I did not make promises of continued employment for the team member.

☐ I have not left out or downplayed any issues to avoid conflict.

☐ I have accurately rated the team member's performance toward established performance expectations (goals and competencies) and have provided performance data to justify my ratings.

☐ I have avoided comments regarding race, ethnicity, gender, sexual orientation, and all other non-job-related characteristics.

☐ I have ensured that my ratings and comments are related to job-specific performance requirements and established performance expectations (goals and competencies).

Sample Performance Appraisal

2017 Performance Appraisal for Pat Smith

Template available for download at www.peakehumancapital.com.

Team Member Information

Last Name: Smith
First Name: Pat
Title: Senior Technical Support Specialist

Review Information

Review Period: 1/1/2017–12/31/2017
Due Date: 2/28/2017

Performance Goals

Use this section to evaluate the team member's performance goals for this review period. For each goal, use the comment area to describe performance expectations, results achieved, and how those results were measured.

1. During the first quarter, receive average rating of 4.0 or above on all customer satisfaction measures.

Manager Rating:	Team Member Rating:
5 = Far exceeds expectations	5 = Far exceeds expectations
4 = Exceeds expectations	4 = Exceeds expectations
3 = Meets expectations	**3 3 = Meets expectations**
2 = Below expectations	2 = Below expectations
1 = Far below expectations	1 = Far below expectations

Manager Comments:	Team Member Comments:
I rated Pat below expectations on this goal. While she worked hard under challenging circumstances, the 4.0 rating was within her control based on the detailed plan we developed to achieve it. Pat focused a bit too much on doing other team members' work and lost focus on achieving her 4.0 customer satisfaction rating.	*I achieved a 3.6 average rating during the first quarter, which was extremely difficult considering my workload and the team's inexperience.*

2. Improve average rating to 4.2 in second quarter.

Manager Rating:	Team Member Rating:
5 = Far exceeds expectations	5 = Far exceeds expectations
4 = Exceeds expectations	4 = Exceeds expectations
3 = Meets expectations	**3 = Meets expectations**
2 = Below expectations	2 = Below expectations
1 = Far below expectations	1 = Far below expectations

Manager Comments:	Team Member Comments:
I rated Pat below expectations on this goal. Once again, she worked very hard but still focused on doing the work of less experienced team members instead of directing them to procedures, tools, and other resources they could use to develop their skills. As a result, Pat was slower than usual responding to customers, which resulted in missing the target of a 4.2 customer satisfaction rating.	*I achieved a 3.8 average rating. My workload got heavier during this period because we had even fewer people on the team than we had during the first quarter. I was the only one left who could answer technical questions. I got positive comments on technical skills from Mr. Lambert, an external customer.*

3. Receive no more than two customer complaints per quarter.

Manager Rating:	Team Member Rating:
5 = Far exceeds expectations	5 = Far exceeds expectations
4 = Exceeds expectations	**4 = Exceeds expectations**
3 = Meets expectations	3 = Meets expectations
2 = Below expectations	2 = Below expectations
1 = Far below expectations	1 = Far below expectations

Manager Comments:	Team Member Comments:
Pat met expectations on this goal— admirable performance in light of the staffing challenges the team faced during the first half of the year. The goal was to receive no more than two complaints per quarter, and Pat was within that range, which was the established goal. In meeting this goal under challenging circumstances, however, Pat exceeded expectations on the Customer Focus competency, which I will comment on in the competencies section below.	*I got two complaints during the first quarter and two during the second quarter. I got only one during the third quarter and one during the fourth quarter. I believe I exceeded the expectations on this goal.*

4. Complete plan for cross-training by February 15.

Manager Rating:	Team Member Rating:
5 = Far exceeds expectations	**5 = Far exceeds expectations**
4 = Exceeds expectations	4 = Exceeds expectations
3 = Meets expectations	3 = Meets expectations
2 = Below expectations	2 = Below expectations
1 = Far below expectations	1 = Far below expectations

Manager Comments:	Team Member Comments:
Under challenging circumstances, Pat completed a robust cross-training plan for the team fourteen days ahead of schedule. The plan was innovative, detailed, and made use of existing materials, online training tools, and other time- and cost-saving approaches that minimized the time and expense needed for the cross-training project. Pat far exceeded expectations on this goal.	*I completed the plan on February 1 (fourteen days ahead of schedule).*

5. Train team in basic technical support by April 15.

Manager Rating:	Team Member Rating:
5 = Far exceeds expectations	5 = Far exceeds expectations
4 = Exceeds expectations	4 = Exceeds expectations
3 = Meets expectations	**3 = Meets expectations**
2 = Below expectations	2 = Below expectations
1 = Far below expectations	1 = Far below expectations

Manager Comments:	Team Member Comments:
Pat met expectations on this goal. She got the team cross-trained by our renegotiated April 1 deadline. Response from the team was positive, and the team's competence increased to a level that lowered overall complaints and increased overall customer satisfaction scores. Thank you for your contribution, Pat.	*Postponed until April 1 because of my extremely heavy technical support workload. Training was thorough and covered all required subjects. People said it was very helpful.*

Competencies

Developing Collaborative Relationships

Develops and uses strategic collaborative relationships to facilitate the accomplishment of work goals between one's area and other areas, teams, departments, business units, and affiliates to help achieve company business goals.

Key Actions:

- Seeks opportunities—learns the organization and proactively tries to build effective working relationships with other people
- Explores partnership opportunities—exchanges information with potential partner areas to clarify partnership benefits and potential problems; collaboratively determines the scope and expectations of the partnerships so that both areas' needs can be met
- Develops others' and own ideas—seeks and expands on original ideas, enhances others' ideas, and contributes own ideas about issues at hand
- Facilitates agreement—gains agreement from partners to support ideas or take partnership-oriented action; uses sound rationale to explain value of actions
- Subordinates own area's goals—places higher priority on company goals than on own area's goals; anticipates effects of own area's actions and decisions on partners; influences others to support partnership objectives
- Builds confidence in others—maintains or enhances self-esteem and self-confidence of peers, team members, and others
- Communicates changes—communicates changes or problems to peers, team members, and others and works on solutions
- Monitors partnership—implements effective means for monitoring and evaluating the partnership process and the attainment of mutual goals

Manager Rating:	Team Member Rating:
5 = Far exceeds expectations	5 = Far exceeds expectations
4 = Exceeds expectations	4 = Exceeds expectations
3 = Meets expectations	**3 = Meets expectations**
2 = Below expectations	2 = Below expectations
1 = Far below expectations	1 = Far below expectations

Manager Comments:	Team Member Comments:
Pat met expectations on this competency as written. I received eleven e-mails during the year complimenting Pat on her people skills—particularly her ability to listen to other people's ideas and collaborate to achieve goals. This is exactly what is expected of a senior technical support specialist. Well done, Pat! I really appreciate your efforts here and their impact on the team's reputation.	*I did well in this area. In November, Dominick Noviello, a member of the team, complimented me for being cooperative.*

Building Trust

Interacts with others in a way that gives them confidence in their intentions and those of the organization.

Key Actions:

- Operates with integrity—demonstrates honesty; keeps commitments; behaves in a consistent manner

- Discloses own positions—shares thoughts, feelings, and rationale so that others understand personal positions

- Remains open to ideas—listens to others and objectively considers others' ideas and opinions, even when they conflict with one's own

- Supports others—treats people with dignity, respect, and fairness; gives proper credit to others; stands up for deserving others and their ideas even in the face of resistance or challenge

- Allows learning from mistakes—allows people to learn from mistakes and encourages new, innovative thinking

Manager Rating:	Team Member Rating:
5 = Far exceeds expectations	5 = Far exceeds expectations
4 = Exceeds expectations	4 = Exceeds expectations
3 = Meets expectations	**3 = Meets expectations**
2 = Below expectations	2 = Below expectations
1 = Far below expectations	1 = Far below expectations

Manager Comments:	Team Member Comments:
Pat met expectations on this competency, demonstrating it as written. As mentioned earlier in this appraisal, I received eleven e-mails this year complimenting Pat on her ability to build rapport and trust—even with challenging customers. Her performance here is in keeping with what is expected of a senior technical support specialist.	*I did well in this area. In November, Jane Taylor, a member of the team, complimented me for being cooperative. I listened to other people's ideas and offered constructive feedback to help them develop.*

Getting Results

Demonstrates accountability for accomplishing objectives; performs successfully on a consistent basis; pushes for results; is bottom-line oriented.

Key Actions:

- Assumes accountability—holds self accountable for fulfilling commitments
- Focuses on what's important—is goal-directed, persistent, driven to achieve objectives; concentrates efforts on the most important priorities; does not get bogged down and become ineffective; can navigate through challenge and difficulty to get the job done
- Takes initiative—is energetic and self-directed; understands what needs to be done and acts accordingly; does not sit and wait to be told what to do; establishes a purpose and vision and establishes a plan to obtain it
- Identifies problems—is skilled at anticipating, identifying, and analyzing problems or roadblocks
- Manages time—uses time effectively and efficiently; concentrates efforts on the most important priorities
- Leverages relationships—leverages strong working relationships with the manager, peers, and clients to get work done
- Keeps customers in mind—identifies customer needs and consistently meets or exceeds their expectations

Manager Rating:	Team Member Rating:
5 = Far exceeds expectations	5 = Far exceeds expectations
4 = Exceeds expectations	**4 = Exceeds expectations**
3 = Meets expectations	3 = Meets expectations
2 = Below expectations	2 = Below expectations
1 = Far below expectations	1 ⊟ Far below expectations

Manager Comments:	Team Member Comments:
Pat met expectations on this competency. While she had a challenging year and worked hard, she struggled a bit during the beginning of the year and missed her customer service targets. Overall, however, she got back on track midyear and, by the end of the year, achieved expected results.	*I got the team trained to handle technical questions from customers. I took the initiative to design, develop, and facilitate the training. The team said they found the training helpful. I also oversaw the task of updating the customer support website.*

Customer Focus

Making customers and their needs a primary focus of one's actions; developing and sustaining productive customer relationships.

Key Actions:

- Seeks to understand customers
- Educates customers
- Builds collaborative relationships
- Takes action to meet customer needs and concerns
- Sets up customer feedback systems

Manager Rating:	Team Member Rating:
5 = Far exceeds expectations	5 = Far exceeds expectations
4 = Exceeds expectations	4 = Exceeds expectations
3 = Meets expectations	**3 = Meets expectations**
2 = Below expectations	2 = Below expectations
1 = Far below expectations	1 = Far below expectations

Manager Comments:	Team Member Comments:
Pat exceeded expectations on this competency as written. Although she did not meet her customer satisfaction targets during the first half of the year, her scores were still relatively high, and she achieved expected performance by year end. In particular, she exceeded expectations by receiving numerous unsolicited positive customer comments—including two from Charlie Evers, a challenging, high-profile customer.	*I built relationships with customers by being up front, honest, and realistic with them. When I could not get back to them as quickly as I wanted to (due to my workload), I apologized and explained the situation in ways they could understand. They have a better understanding of how hard our team works.*

Final Comments (Optional)	
Manager's Final Comments:	**Team Member's Final Comments:**

Overall Ratings	
Goal Section Rating *(Sum of goal ratings divided by number of goals, rounded up)*	**3.0**
Competencies Section Rating *(Sum of competency ratings divided by number of competencies, rounded up)*	**3.3**
Overall Rating *(Sum of goal and competencies section ratings divided by two and rounded up; goals and competencies sections each make up 50 percent of the overall rating)*	**3.2**

Signatures

By signing this document, you acknowledge that your manager has discussed it with you. Signing this document does not indicate that you agree with its content. You may add additional comments in the final comments section above, if desired.

Team Member Signature:	Date:
Pat Smith	*January 15, 2017*
Manager Signature:	Date:
Terry Sanders	*January 15, 2017*

Step Four: Prepare for the Appraisal Meeting

At its most effective, the appraisal meeting is a two-way conversation between you and the team member. It is a discussion of the team member's performance during the entire year based on established expectations and actual performance toward those expectations.

To prepare for the appraisal meeting,

- choose a time and place for the meeting and inform the team member;

- send the team member a copy of the appraisal meeting agenda, if desired (see page 74);

- encourage the team member to complete a self-appraisal or to come prepared to share his or her views of his or her performance; and

- ensure that the appraisal meeting space is quiet, private, and free of disruptions.

Step Five: Conduct the Appraisal Meeting

The appraisal meeting is the culmination of your yearlong performance management efforts. It is your opportunity to accurately summarize the team member's entire year of performance, praise and thank the team member for good performance, discuss ideas for improving performance during the coming year, and identify areas in which the team member can enhance competencies (knowledge, skills, and abilities).

Because appraisal meetings are most often conducted behind closed doors, with only the manager and team member present, most managers never get feedback on how effectively they conduct these meetings. To ensure that you are conducting your appraisal meetings as effectively as possible be sure to

- schedule sufficient time for the meeting (an hour is usually enough);

- inform the team member of the meeting time and place in advance;

- silence phones, e-mail notifications, and other distractions before the meeting;

- follow an agenda, such as the one on the next page, to manage time and stay on track; and

- make the meeting a two-way conversation, giving the team member opportunities to explain his or her point of view and to develop ideas for enhanced future performance, if appropriate.

The tools on the following pages provide guidelines.

Appraisal Meeting Agenda

- ☐ Make introductory remarks, and thank the team member for participating in the appraisal process.

- ☐ Use the information below to explain how the appraisal meeting will be conducted.

- ☐ Give the team member a copy of the appraisal so he or she can follow along.

- ☐ Review each goal and competency. On each goal and competency, let the team member give his or her rating and comments first, then share yours.

  – Compare actual results with expectations.

  – Be honest.

  – If your rating is lower or higher than the team member's, discuss why.

  – Give the team member insight into your thought process, and provide sufficient, relevant, and accurate data and examples that justify your rating.

  – Use the phrase "for example…" when illustrating how the team member performed; then provide specific examples to justify your ratings.

  – Change your rating if the team member provides additional data that justify the change.

  – If you choose not to change your rating, explain why; be sure the performance data justify your decision.

  – Give the team member feedback about performance that needs to improved, if warranted.

  – Avoid comments about race, age, gender, or national origin.

- ☐ End on a positive note by thanking the team member for his or her time, openness, and/or performance, as appropriate.

Phase Three: Appraise Performance—Key Points

1. Base performance appraisals on expectations (goals and competencies) established at the beginning of the performance year and adjusted during the year as appropriate.

2. Encourage team members to complete a self-appraisal on established goals and competencies to promote a perception of fairness and to get the team member's point of view.

3. Rate each competency and goal individually. Use performance data collected throughout the year (sales figures, call records, observed behavior, feedback given and received, coaching conversations documented, etc.) to justify your ratings. Provide specific examples.

4. Base ratings on performance documented throughout the entire performance year.

5. Check the appraisal for rating errors, personal biases, and legally questionable wording. Correct these as needed.

6. Deliver the appraisal in real time (preferably in person) so that you can provide context and explain your ratings and comments.

Phase Four: Plan Your Development

Desired Outcomes

- Identification of strong competencies that can be made stronger and weak competencies that can be improved

- Creation of a competency-based development with one to four SMART goals focused on developing one or two competencies

A senior-level director at my company recently complained to me about being passed over for a promotion to a role for which she was a favored candidate. The conversation went something like this:

Director:	This is so frustrating. I was told I was a strong future candidate for an executive role, but once again, I was passed over, and the company filled the position from the outside.
Me:	I don't blame you for being frustrated. Do you have any idea why you were not promoted?
Director:	I was told that I'm still a strong future candidate based on my performance in my current role but that I'm still not ready for promotion to the executive level.
Me:	What have you done to become ready for promotion to the executive level?
Director:	I've taken some classes and worked hard in my current position. I've also asked my boss for ideas on how to develop, but he hasn't followed up with me on that.
Me:	Are you clear on what it takes to be ready for promotion to the executive level?
Director:	Not as clear as I need to be, apparently.
Me:	My team can help you with that. Let's look at the competencies you'll need to be ready for the executive level and work with your boss to create a plan for developing those competencies while you are in your current role.

While development can (and does) take place organically, going at it without a plan is like looking for ripe fruit in the wild instead of planting and cultivating fruit trees. While organic development certainly has its value, it is usually not sufficient. On the pages that follow, we will look at how to augment organic development with a development plan focused on developing the competencies (knowledge, skills, and abilities) needed for success in a current or future role.

You may have noticed that this phase of the performance management process is called "Plan Your Development." This phrasing is deliberate. Development planning works best when the plan is created and owned by the person being developed. This approach fosters involvement and motivation in the person being developed and leads to a higher rate of development plan success.

Plan Your Development: Some Additional Wisdom

The greatest danger for most of us is not that our aim is too high and we miss it, but that it is too low and we reach it.

—Michelangelo

The meeting of preparation with opportunity generates the offspring we call luck.

—Tony Robbins

The discipline of writing something down is the first step toward making it happen.

—Lee Iaccoca

A development plan is most effective when it focuses on making strong competencies stronger. Weaknesses should be strengthened only if they are holding the team member back in his or her current position or one to which he or she aspires.

Allow the team member to lead the creation of his or her development—with your involvement, guidance, and support. This approach promotes engagement in the process and reinforces the message that the team member is ultimately responsible for his or her own development. Provide the team member with the directions and templates that follow. Make yourself available to answer questions, and provide developmental ideas as needed.

There are five steps to creating an effective development plan:

- Step one: Consider business goals
- Step two: Identify competencies necessary for success
- Step three: Choose competencies to develop now
- Step four: Write a development goal for each competency
- Step five: Finalize your development plan

Let's take a closer look at each step.

Step One: Consider Business Goals

Before constructing a development plan, it is important to gather the information you needed to make sound development decisions. The team member's assigned performance expectations (goals and competencies) are the starting point for gathering this information.

List your current business goals below. Goals should be **SMART** (Specific, Measurable, Achievable, Relevant, and Time-bound).

Business Goal	Deadline
Example: By November 30, 2017, negotiate a contract with a performance management software vendor that provides the software at or below the amount allocated in the departmental budget.	*November 30, 2017*

Step Two: Identify Competencies Necessary for Success

List the competencies (knowledge, skills, and abilities) necessary for successful completion of the business goals listed. A good competency reference book, such as *For Your Development* by Michael M. Lombardo, will provide several from which to choose.

Competency	Why Is It Necessary?
Example: Negotiation	*I need intermediate-level negotiation skills to effectively negotiate the performance management software contract.*

Next, determine which of the competencies listed above are currently strengths and which are currently weaknesses.

Competency	Strength or Weakness? Why?
Example: Negotiation	*Weakness because I have no negotiation skills or experience.*

Step Three: Choose Competencies to Develop Now

To ensure that the development plan is manageable, focus on developing only one or two competencies at a time for a period of three to six months. This will allow time to gain the in-depth knowledge and experience needed for true competency development.

Identify one or two competencies to be developed during the next three to six months.

Competencies Identified for Development (Maximum of Two)
Example: Negotiation

Step Four: Write a Development Goal for Each Competency

Use the space on the next page to write no more than two development goals, including action steps and deadlines. If two competencies have been selected for development, write one goal for each. If only one competency has been selected for development, write one or two goals for developing that competency. Make sure the development goals are SMART (Specific, Measurable, Achievable, Relevant, and Time-bound).

Developmental Goal	Action Steps and Deadlines
Example: Develop intermediate-level negotiation skills by September 30, 2017.	*Complete American Management Association's negotiation workshop by July 31, 2017.*
	Colead negotiation of the learning management vendor contract by September 15, 2017, applying knowledge gained at the negotiation workshop.
	Lead negotiation of the performance management software vendor contract by December 1, 2017, applying knowledge gained at the negotiation workshop.

Developmental Goal #1	Action Steps and Deadlines

Developmental Goal #2 (Optional)	Action Steps and Deadlines

Step Five: Finalize Your Development Plan

Discuss the development goals you created on the preceding pages with your manager. After the discussion, make adjustments as needed. Use the template on pages 84–85 to finalize your development plan.

Development Plan for Success in Current Role

Name:

Plan Start Date:

Plan End Date:

1. What are my career goals?

2. What specific on-the job experiences do I need during the next year to achieve my career goals?

3. What development goals will I set to make sure I get these on-the-job experiences? *(If you include reading books or taking classes to gain knowledge, include how you will apply that knowledge through on-the-job experiences.)*

Development Goal #1	Action Steps and Deadlines

Development Goal #2 (Optional)	Action Steps and Deadlines

4. What abilities (competencies/skills) will I develop through these on-the-job experiences?

5. How will I measure my progress?

6. How will I know that this development plan was successful?

7. What support do I need from my manager for this plan to be successful?

Additional Notes:

_____

Team Member's Signature: *Date:*

Manager's Signature: *Date:*

Development Planning for Career Growth

Overview

The development planning approach on the preceding pages focuses on developing competencies needed for meeting performance expectations in a team member's current role. The guidelines on the pages that follow use the same general principles to create a development plan for career growth.

When done effectively, a career growth development plan balances individual career needs and interests with the company's strategy and work requirements. These development plans are most effective when the team member and manager collaborate to create them.

Objective

You will create your development plan by following these five steps:

1. Assess your competency strengths and weaknesses
2. Get others' assessments of your competency strengths and weaknesses
3. Select one or two competencies to develop
4. Determine possible methods for developing these competencies
5. Create a competency development plan for the position you desire

Step One: Assess Your Competency Strengths and Weaknesses

Step One Overview

During this step, you will familiarize yourself with the competencies (knowledge, skills, and abilities) necessary for success in the position you desire.

Step One Actions

☐ Familiarize yourself with the competencies (knowledge, skills, and abilities) necessary for success in the position you desire. For guidance, ask people currently in the position and refer to a competency guide book such as *For Your Improvement* by Michael M. Lombardo.

☐ From your own point of view, which of these competencies are your strongest? Which are your weakest? List these competencies on the worksheet on page 92.

☐ Consider which competencies you may need to develop further. Think about strengths you can make stronger or weaknesses that are holding you back. Think about why these competencies should be developed. List these competencies on the worksheet on page 93.

How I See Myself

My Strongest Competencies

From your own point of view, which of the competencies necessary for success in the position you desire are your strongest?

My Weakest Competencies

From your own point of view, which of the competencies necessary for success in the position you desire are your weakest?

How I See Myself

Competencies to Develop

Competency	Why Should It Be Developed?

Step Two: Get Others' Assessments of Your Competency Strengths and Weaknesses

Step Two Overview

During this step, you will also have conversations with your upline managers, peers, and people currently in the role you desire to gain their deeper insights and suggestions for your development. When you have completed this step, you will have the information you need to identify the competencies most important for your development.

Step Two Actions

☐ Review your most recent performance appraisal.

– From the point of view of the manager who completed your appraisal, which competencies are your strongest? Which are your weakest? List these competencies on the worksheet on page 95.

☐ Schedule and conduct conversations with your manager and at least one person who is in the position you desire. Get their input on your competency strengths, weaknesses, and developmental areas. Ask for suggestions on how you can develop these competencies in your current role. List the key points from these interviews on the worksheets on pages 96–98.

Suggested Interview Questions:

1. Based on what you have seen me do, what are my strongest competencies?

2. Specifically, what have you seen me do that makes you feel these are my strongest competencies?

3. Based on what you have seen me do, what are my weakest competencies?

4. Specifically, what have you seen me do that makes you feel these are my weakest competencies?

5. Which of my strong competencies are most important for me to make even stronger to succeed in the position I desire? Why are these competencies important for me to develop?

6. Which of my weaker competencies have the potential to hold me back in the position I desire? Why are these competencies important for me to develop?

7. What are some ways in which I can develop these competencies day to day in my current role?

☐ From these individuals' points of view, which strong competencies should you make stronger? Which weak ones are holding you back? Why should you develop these competencies? How could you develop them on a day-to-day basis in your current role? Include the answers to these questions on the worksheets on pages 96–98.

How Others See Me

Strongest Competencies on My Performance Appraisal

Review your most recent performance appraisal. Based on this appraisal, which competencies are your strongest? *(Skip this step if you do not have a current performance appraisal.)*

Weakest Competencies on My Performance Appraisal

Review your most recent performance appraisal. Based on this appraisal, which competencies are your weakest? *(Skip this step if you do not have a current performance appraisal.)*

Competencies to Develop for the Position I Desire

In the space provided below, note the *key points* from your manager interview.

Manager

Competency to Develop	Why Should It Be Developed?	How Could It Be Developed in My Current Role?

Competencies to Develop for the Position I Desire

In the space provided below, note the *key points* from your interview with a person in the role you desire.

Someone Already in the Role

Competency to Develop	Why Should It Be Developed?	How Could It Be Developed in My Current Role?

Competencies to Develop for the Position I Desire

(Optional) In the space provided below, note the *key points* from your interview with a second person in the role you desire.

Someone Already in the Role

Competency to Develop	Why Should It Be Developed?	How Could It Be Developed in My Current Role?

Step Three: Select One or Two Competencies to Develop

Step Three Overview

During this step, you will select one or two competencies to develop during the next six months. Selecting a small number of competencies will help you focus more deeply in these key areas and ensure that your individual development plan is achievable. When you have completed this step, you will be ready to create a detailed individual development plan.

Step Three Actions

☐ Review the information you collected about your competency strengths and weaknesses (pages 92–98).

☐ Based on your own assessment and the feedback you received, select one or two competencies to develop during the next six months.

☐ List these competencies in the space provided on pages 100–101. Include opportunities for developing these competencies within the scope of your current role.

Selecting Competencies to Develop

Select one or two competencies to develop during the next six months. Selecting a small number of competencies will help you focus more deeply in these key areas and ensure that your individual development plan is achievable.

Competency #1

Competency to Develop

Why Should It Be Developed?

How Can I Develop It within the Scope of My Current Role?

Selecting Competencies to Develop

If desired, select an additional competency to develop during the next six months.

Competency #2

Competency to Develop

Why Should It Be Developed?

How Can I Develop It within the Scope of My Current Role?

Step Four: Determine Methods for Developing Competencies

Step Four Overview

During this step, you will determine possible methods for developing the competencies required for success in the position you desire. When you have completed this step, you will have determined methods for gaining the skills you need and applying them on the job. This approach will allow you to develop the skills you need in the most effective way possible—through actual experience.

While training can be useful for development, it is not always the most appropriate or cost-effective approach. Consider the list of additional development options below:

- guided reading
- partnerships with other employees
- stretch assignments
- extracurricular activities
- internal education and training
- e-Learning
- external coursework
- teaching others

Place most of your focus on identifying the on-the-job experiences needed to become ready for the position you desire.

Step Four Actions

1. Review the competencies you selected for development on pages 100–101.

2. Using the worksheets on pages 103–105, list methods for developing the competencies you selected. Consider the following questions:

   - How will you gain the competency-related knowledge you need?

   - How will you apply this knowledge on the job to develop each competency?

Determining Methods for Developing Competencies

___

Instructions

Use the worksheets on pages 103–105 to list methods for developing the competencies you selected on pages 100–101. Consider the following questions:

1. How will you gain the competency-related knowledge you need?

2. What on-the-job experiences do you need to apply the knowledge and develop the competency?

List general approaches for now. You will get more specific during the next step. An example is provided below.

EXAMPLE

Competency to Develop

Innovating

Methods for Gaining Knowledge	**On-the-Job Experiences for Applying Knowledge**
– *Read reputable books and articles on business innovation (e.g., by Harvard Business School)*	– *Volunteer for special assignments or projects that require generating new product ideas or revamping current processes*
– *Interview people who have implemented successful and creative ideas, products, processes, and so forth, and analyze what made them successful*	– *Identify barriers (personal, departmental, organizational) to innovation; then develop and implement a plan to eliminate them*
– *Benchmark innovation practices used by other companies and analyze what made them successful or unsuccessful*	– *Identify a significant product or process within my span of influence that can be significantly improved. Partner with someone skilled at innovation to develop and implement product or process innovations*
– *Take a reputable online course on business innovation*	

Determining Methods for Developing Competencies

Competency #1

Competency to Develop

Methods for Gaining Knowledge

On-the-Job Experiences for Applying Knowledge

Determining Methods for Developing Competencies

Competency #2

Competency to Develop

Methods for Gaining Knowledge

On-the-Job Experiences for Applying Knowledge

Step Five: Create a Competency Development Plan for the Position You Desire

Step Five Overview

During this step, you will create an actionable plan to develop the competencies you selected in step three of this process. When you complete this step, you will have written one or two SMART (Specific, Measurable, Achievable, Relevant, and Time-bound) development goals—each with five to ten specific tasks. This approach will allow you to focus deeply on the most important competencies necessary for your development. The time line for your development plan will be three to six months.

Your development plan should focus primarily on making your strong competencies stronger. Weaknesses should be addressed only if they are holding you back from the position you desire.

As you write your development plan, consider how you can develop the competencies you selected within your current role (e.g., volunteering for additional projects, developing an innovative solution to a problem your department is facing, etc.).

Step Five Actions

- ☐ Review the competencies you selected for development (pages 100–101).

- ☐ Review the methods you identified for gaining and applying competency-related knowledge (pages 104–105).

- ☐ Review your current performance goals and/or job responsibilities.

- ☐ Use the worksheets on pages 111–113 to list the competencies you have chosen to develop for your future role and the actions you will take to develop those competencies. Be sure to include a due date for each action. An example is provided on pages 107–110.

Managing Performance for Results

Creating a Development Plan for a Role You Desire

Using the worksheets on pages 111–113, write one or two SMART (Specific, Measurable, Achievable, Relevant, and Time-bound) development goals, including tasks and deadlines. You will find an example below.

Example

Development Plan for a Role You Desire

Name: Frieda Livery **Plan Start Date:** 2/1/2017 **Plan End Date:** 8/31/2017

1. For what future role am I developing?

   Director, Human Resources

2. What are the one or two competencies most important to develop now to prepare for my future role?

   Executive Presence

   Leading Organizational Change

3. For each competency, how will I gain the additional knowledge I need? Once I have gained that knowledge, how will I apply it in my current role to gain experience?

Competency #1	Actions for Gaining and Applying Knowledge
Leading Organizational Change	*Discuss change leadership practices and real-world experiences with two directors or executives who have done this successfully within the organization* **(by 3/31/2017)** *Review change management best practices from Corporate Leadership Council or another credible source* **(by 4/30/2017)** *Lead the transition from the current human resources information system to the new one across departments, functions, and leadership levels* **(by 8/31/2017)**

Competency #2 (Optional)	Actions for Gaining and Applying Knowledge
Executive Presence	*Serve as go-to person for VP Human Resources on the transition to the new human resources information system* **(throughout 2017)** *Attend senior executive meetings monthly; discuss approaches for achieving company business goals; provide updates on implementation of new human resources information system* **(throughout 2017)**

4. How will I measure my progress?

   Monthly progress meetings with VP Human Resources

   Successful achievement of development goals (listed above) within established time frames

5. What support do I need from my manager for this plan to be successful?

   Monthly access to senior executive meetings

   Meetings every two weeks to discuss progress, plan approaches, and receive coaching and feedback

Additional Notes:

Team Member's
Signature: *Frieda Livery*   Date: *1/15/2017*

Manager's Signature: *I. M. Alleder*   Date: *1/15/2017*

Development Plan for a Role You Desire

Name:

Plan Start Date:

Plan End Date:

1. For what future role am I developing?

2. What are the one or two competencies most important to develop now to prepare for my future role?

3. For each competency, how will I gain the additional knowledge I need? Once I have gained that knowledge, how will I apply it in my current role to gain experience?

Competency #1	Actions for Gaining and Applying Knowledge

Competency #2 (Optional)	Actions for Gaining and Applying Knowledge

4. How will I measure my progress?

5. What support do I need from my manager for this plan to be successful?

Additional Notes:

_____

*Team Member's
Signature:*   *Date:*

Manager's Signature: *Date:*

Phase Four: Plan Your Development—Key Points

1. Focus development plans on building competencies needed for success in your current role or to prepare for a future role you desire.

2. Focus on making strong competencies stronger. Focus on developing weak competencies only if they are preventing success in your current role or if they would prevent you from moving into the role you desire.

3. Develop no more than two competencies at a time over a three-to-six-month period. Depth is more effective than breadth.

4. For each competency you wish to develop, focus on two things: how you will gain the additional knowledge you need and how you will apply that knowledge on the job to develop competence. Both are critical.

5. Write your development plan in the form of one SMART (Specific, Measurable, Achievable, Relevant, and Time-bound) goal per competency. Include the specific actions you will take to gain the knowledge you need and to apply that knowledge on the job.

In Closing

There are many variations of performance management in use at organizations around the world. They vary considerably in many ways, but the most effective ones consistently adhere to the four key elements of performance management.

1. Set expectations.
2. Review progress toward expectations.
3. Appraise performance against expectations.
4. Plan for future skill development.

Regardless of the approach you take to manage your team's performance, stick to these elements and you will significantly enhance your team's performance and your effectiveness as a manager.

For additional guidance on effective performance management, visit www.peakehumancapital.com.